The Social Welfare Word Book

Michelle McNally

Other titles from Longman include:

On Becoming a Manager in Social Work edited by Barbara Hearn, Giles Darvill and Beth Morris
Quality Assurance for Social Care Agencies by Emlyn Cassam and Himu Gupta
Making the Best Use of Consultants by Philip Hope
How to Organise Conferences, Workshops and Training Events by Alan Dearling
Getting Started with NVQ: Tackling the Integrated Care Awards by Barry Meteyard
Caring in the Community: A Networking Approach to Community Partnership by Steve Trevillion
NSPCC: *Child Sexual Abuse: Listening, Hearing and Validating the Experiences of Children* by Corinne Wattam, John Hughes and Harry Blagg
NSPCC: *Listening to Children: The Professional Response to Hearing the Abused Child* edited by Anne Bannister, Kevin Barrett, and Eileen Shearer
NSPCC: *From Hearing to Healing: Working with the Aftermath of Child Sexual Abuse* edited by Anne Bannister
NSPCC: *Making a Case in Child Protection* by Corinne Wattam
NSPCC: *Key Issues in Child Protection for Health Visitors and Nurses* edited by Jane Naish and Christopher Cloke
Making Sense of the Children Act (2nd edition) by Nick Allen
Coping with Violent Behaviour: A Handbook for Social Work Staff by Eric R. Brady
Working with Disaster edited by Tim Newburn
Community Care Keyworker Manual by Barry Meteyard
Staff Supervision in Social Care by Tony Morrison

Social Services Training Manuals

First Line Management: Staff by Kevin Ford and Sarah Hargreaves
Effective Use of Teambuilding by Alan Dearling
Manual on Elder Abuse by Chris Phillipson and Simon Biggs
Developing Training Skills by Tim Pickles, Howie Armstrong and Bruce Britton
Training for Mental Health by Thurstine Basset and Elaine Burrel
Monitoring and Evaluation in the Social Services by David and Suzanne Thorpe
Child Protection Training Manual by Brenda Green, Sissi Loftin and Paul Saunders

The Social Welfare Word Book

by

Alan Dearling

Published by Longman Information and Reference, Longman Group UK Ltd,
6th Floor, Westgate House, The High, Harlow, Essex CM20 1YR, England and
Associated Companies throughout the world.

A catalogue record for this book is available from The British Library.

ISBN 0–582–21976–0

Typeset by The Midlands Book Typesetting Company Limited,
Loughborough, Leicestershire

Printed in Great Britain by Redwood Books,
Trowbridge, Wiltshire

The Social Welfare
Word Book

CONTENTS

Acknowledgements

Any attempt to write a dictionary is bound to be a collaborative process. It is inevitably a distillation of many other people's ideas, writing and professional practice. This Word Book came about as a result of my colleague, John Harper at Longman's, suggesting that it might be something I could do in odd moments on the long train journey from Axminster to Waterloo. Ron Lynam at Bookstall Services in Derby confirmed that there was a need for an up-to-date guide to social welfare terms and professional jargon. Rather naively I agreed to compile the book for Longman, and with hindsight it has proved to be the hardest book I have ever tried to write. I suspect that my official 'readers', Chris Payne, Director of the Social Care Centre for Practice and Staff Development (NISW/SCA), and Geraldine Peacock, Director of the National Autistic Society, probably now wish they had never offered to help me wade through the ever-growing sea of specialist language and acronyms!

As far as possible I have tried to provide definitions, information on the contexts in which words are used, and some commentary on contradictory meanings. Geraldine, Chris and other colleagues such as Alan Taylor from Apex Trust, Sing Siong Teoh and Theresa Thomson offered valuable advice and criticism of the words for inclusion, but the final decisions on what to include were mine alone. I am very grateful to them for their help, and to editor Kate Lodge, Jacqueline Jones for helping to type the various drafts of the manuscript and Jason O'Donnell for managing to maintain a sense of humour while photocopying hundreds of entries. There are no definitive descriptions of social welfare words, but hopefully the Word Book will help students, workers and writers grapple with some of the complexities, and at times peculiarities, of the words and meanings that are used in the widely divergent settings of the social welfare world. Over the next few years I am sure that new words and meanings will evolve. No doubt I will also hear of mistakes I have made in this first edition of the Word Book – if you have any comments on the entries, please feel free to contact me through Longman Information and Reference Division.

Finally, my thanks to Christine, my partner, for her patience with me while I was researching and writing the book.

Alan Dearling
May 1993

Acronyms and Abbreviations

AA	Alcoholics Anonymous
AA	Attendance Allowance
AASW	Advanced Award in Social work
ABH	Actual bodily harm
ABSWAP	Association of Black Social Workers and Allied Professions
ACAS	Advisory, Conciliation and Arbitration Service
ACC	Association of County Councils
ACE	Age Concern England
ACENVU	Association of Chief Executives of National Voluntary Organisations
ACHE	Association of Community Home Schools
ACOP	Association of Chief Officers of Probation
ACPO	Assistant Chief Probation Officer
ACPO	Association of Chief Probation Officers
ACRE	Action with Communities in Rural England
ACS	Age Concern Scotland
ACT	Action centred learning
ACT	Assessment and counselling team
ACW	Age Concern Wales
ACW	Association of Community Workers
ADC	Association of District Councils
ADSS	Association of Directors of Social Services – England and Wales
ADSW	Association of Directors of Social Work – Scotland
AHA	Area Health Authority
AID	Artificial Insemination – Donor
AIH	Artificial Insemination – Husband
AIDs	Acquired Immune Deficiency Syndrome
AJJ	Association of Juvenile Justice
ALACE	Association of Local Authority Chief Executives
ALBSU	Adult Literacy Basic Skills Unit
AMA	Association of Metropolitan Authorities
APA	Accreditation of Prior Achievement
APL	Accreditation of Prior Learning
APR	Annual percentage rate of change
ARC	Action Resource Centre
ARC	Association for Residential Care
ARMS	Multiple Sclerosis Research Ltd
ASCT	Association of Social Care Tutors
ASH	Action on Smoking and Heath
ASSET	Assistance towards employment centre
ATC	Adult Training Centre
ATSWE	Association of Teachers in Social Work Education
AVERT	AIDs Education and Research Trust

BAAF	British Agencies for Adoption and Fostering
BAC	British Association for Counselling
BACIE	British Association for Commercial and Industrial Education
BADCO	British Association of Domiciliary Care Officers
BAS	British Association of Settlements and Social Action Centres
BASW	British Association of Social Workers
BATOD	British Association of Teachers of the Deaf
BC	Borough Council
BCODP	British Council of Organisations of Disabled People
BDA	British Deaf Association
BFCHP	British Association of Care Home Proprietors
BHAN	Black HIV and AIDs Network
BIM	British Institute of Management
BIMH	British Institute of Mental Handicap
BIOSS	British Institute of Organisation and Social Studies
BITC	Business in the Community
BLESMA	British Limbless Ex-Servicemen's Association
BMA	British Medical Association
BPS	British Psychological Society
BRCS	British Red Cross Society
BS	British Standards
BSL	British Sign Language
BSMT	British Society for Music Therapy
BTEC	Business and Technician Education Council
BUSWE	British Union of Social Work Employees
BYC	British Youth Council
CA	Children Act 1989
CAB	Citizens Advice Bureau
CAL	Computer Assisted Learning
CALIBRE	Cassette Library for the Blind and Disabled
CAO	Child Assessment Order
CAP	Christian Action on Poverty
CAPT	Child Accident Prevention Trust
CARE	CARE for Mentally Handicapped People
CATS	Credit Accumulation and Transfer Scheme
CAWTU	Church Action with the Unemployed
CB	Child Benefit
CBI	Confederation of British Industry
CC	County Council
CCETSW	Central Council for Education and Training in Social Work
CCP	Chief Crown Prosecutor
CCPO	Conference of Chief Probation Officers

CCPR	Central Council of Physical Recreation
CCT	Compulsory Competitive Tendering
CCTA	City College for Technology and the Arts
CEO	Chief Education Officer
CGLI	City and Guilds London Institute
CH	Children's Homes
CH	Community Home
CHAR	Housing Campaign for Single People
CHAS	Catholic Housing Aid Society
CHC	Community Health Centre
CHE	Campaign for Homosexual Equality
CHE	Community Home (Education)
Child Care	Formerly National Council of Voluntary Child Care Organisations
CCO	Child Care Officer
CEEFAX	BBC TV teletext service
CI	Community Industry
CIA	Critical Incident Analysis
CIOB	Chartered Institute of Builders
CJ	Criminal justice
CJA	Criminal Justice Act
CMHC	Community Mental Health Centre
CMHT	Community Mental Health Team
COI	Central Office of Information
COSLA	Convention of Scottish Local Authorities
CoHSE	Confederation of Health Service Employees
CP	Community Programme
CPA	Centre for Policy on Ageing
CPAG	Child Poverty Action Group
CPF	Community Projects Foundation
CPN	Community Psychiatric Nurse
CPO	Chief Probation Officer
CPS	Centre for Policy Studies
CPS	Crown Prosecution Service
CPVE	Certificate of Pre-Vocational Education
CQSW	Certificate of Qualification in Social Work
CRC	Community Relations Council
CRE	Commission for Racial Equality
CRO	Community Relations Officer
CRUSE	Bereavement Care organisation
CSA	Child Support Agency
CSBF	Civil Service Benevolent Fund
CSC	Care Sector Consortium
CSCS	Commonwealth Students' Children Society

CSO	Community Service Order (or Officer)
CSS	Certificate in Social Service
CSS	Council of Social Service
CSSP	Catholic Social Services for Prisoners
CSV	Community Service Volunteers
CSWB	Certificate for Social Workers with the Blind
CSWD	Certificate for Social Workers with the Deaf
CTC	City technology college
CTLD	Community Team for People with Learning Difficulties
CWO	Court Welfare Officer
CYPA	Children and Young Persons Act 1969
CYWU	Community and Youth Workers Union
D of E	Department of Employment
DA	Disability allowance
DAIS	Drug Advice and Information Service
DAO	Duly authorised officer
DC	District Council
DCPO	Deputy Chief Probation Officer
DET	Disability Equality Training
DFE	Department for Education
DGGA	Distressed Gentlefolk Aid Association
DGM	District General Manager
DH	Department of Health
DHA	District Health Authority
DIAL UK	National Association of Disablement Information and Advice Lines
DIG	Disablement Income Group
DipSW	Diploma in Social Work
DLA	Disability Living Allowance
DLF	Disablement Living Foundation
DMU	Directly Managed Unit (non-Trust NHS provider unit)
DoE	Department of the Environment
DoE	Duke of Edinburgh's Award Scheme
DPP	Director of Public Prosecutions
DRO	Disablement Rehabilitation Officer
DRT	Disability Resource Team
DSO	Direct Service Organisation
DSS	Department of Social Security
DSS	Director of Social Service
DTI	Department of Trade and Industry
EA	Employment Action
EAS	Enterprise Allowance Scheme

EBD	Emotional and Behavioural Difficulties
EC	European Community
EC	European Court
ECCTIS	Educational Counselling and Credit Transfer Information Service
ECHO	European Confederation of Care Home Owners
ED	Employment Development
EEC	European Economic Community
EEG	Employment and Enterprise Group
EFL	English as a foreign language
EGAS	Educational Grants Advisory Service
EHE	Enterprise in higher education initiative
ENB	English National Board for Nursing
EO	Equal Opportunities
EOC	Equal Opportunities Commission
EOP	Equal Opportunities Policy
EPA	Educational Priority Area
EPA	Evidence from past achievements
EPH	Elderly People's Home
EPIC	Educational Policy Information Centre
EPO	Emergency Protection Order
ERC	Employment Rehabilitation Centre
ERS	Employment Rehabilitation Service
ES	Employment Service
ESF	European Social Fund
ESO	Education Supervision Order
ESRC	Economic and Social Research Council
ET	Employment Training
ETI	Education and Training Initiative
ETS	Education and Trading Standards
EW	Education Welfare
EWO	Educational Welfare Officer
FAIR	Family Action, Information and Rescue
FC	Family Credit
FCU	Federation of Claimants Unions
FCWTG	Federation of Community Work Training Groups
FHSA	Family Health Service Authority
FIAC	Federation of Independent Advice Centres
FIS	Family Income Supplement
FPA	Family Planning Association
FPC	Family Practitioner Committee
FR	Family review
FREE	Forum on the Rights of Elderly People to Education

FRG	Family Rights Group
FSU	Family Service Unit
FUMPO	Federated Union of Managerial and Professional Officers
FWA	Family Welfare Association
GAL	Guardian Ad Litem
GAPS	Group for the Advancement of Psychotherapy and Psychodynamics
GBH	Grievous bodily harm
GCSE	General Certificate of Secondary Education
GLAD	Greater London Association for Disabled People
GLAD	Gay and Lesbian Legal Advice
GP	General Practitioner
GPMH	Good Practice in Mental Health
GRTA	Group Relations Training Association
HA	Health Authority
HA	Housing associations
HAG	Housing Association Grant
HAPA	Handicapped Adventure Playground Association
HAT	Housing Action Trust
HB	Housing Benefit
HC	Housing Corporation
HEADWAY	National Head Injuries Association
HEC	Health Education Council
HERA	Housing Employment Register and Advice
HIV	Human Immuno-deficiency virus
HMI	Her Majesty's Inspector (of Education) (see OFSTED)
HMO	Houses in multiple occupation
HMP	Her Majesty's Prison
HMSO	Her Majesty's Stationery Office
HO	Home Office
HP	Hire Purchase
HRA	Housing Revenue Account
HSA	Housing Studies Association
HSE	Health and Safety Executive
HTNT	High technology national training
HtA	Help the Aged
HUG	House user group
HV	Health Visitor
HVA	Health Visitors Association
IASSW	International Association of Schools of Social Work
ICA	Invalidity Care Allowance

ICAN	Invalid Children's Aid Nationwide
ICG	Institute of Careers Guidance
ICP	Individual care plan
IFSW	International Federation of Social Workers
IHSM	Institute of Health Service Management
ILS	Independent Living Scheme
IoH	Institute of Housing
IMPACT	International Initiative Against Avoidable Disablement
IPM	Institute of Personnel Management
IS	Income support
ISDD	Institute for the Study of Drug Dependence
ISR	Individual service review
ISS	International Social Service
ISTD	Institute for the Study and Treatment of Delinquency
IT	Information Technology
IT	Intermediate Technology
IT	Intermediate Treatment
ITO	Intermediate Treatment Officer
ITU	Industrial Therapy Unit
IV	Interactive video
IVS	International Voluntary Service
JC	Job Centre
JCC	Joint Care Committee
JCWI	Joint Council for the Welfare of Immigrants
JIGS	Job Interview Guarantee Scheme
JNC	Joint Negotiating Committee
JP	Justice of the Peace
JTS	Job Training Scheme
JUC	Joint Universities Council for Social and Public Administration
KCN	Kids Club Network
KFC	King's Fund Centre
LAG	Legal Action Group
LARRIE	Local Authority Race Relations Information Exchange
LASS	Local Authority Social Services
LB	London Borough
LBA	London Boroughs Association
LBTC	London Based Training Consortium: London Training for Care
LD	Learning difficulty/disability
LEA	Local Education Authority
LGMB	Local Government Management Board

LIB	Lead Industry Body
LIPS	Law Improvement Programme
LSVT	Large scale voluntary transfer (of stock)
LVSC	London Voluntary Service Council
LWROG	London Welfare Rights Offices Group
MA	Mobility Allowance
MACA	Mental After Care Association
MAMA	Meet a Mum Association
MARCH	Association for Mental After Care in Registered Homes
MATCH	Mothers Apart from their Children
MBO	Management by objectives
MBO	Management buy-out
MDC	Metropolitan District Council
MDG	Muscular Dystrophy Group
MDO	Mentally Disordered Offenders
ME	Myalgic Encephalomyelitis
MECS	Mobile Emergency Care Service
MENCAP	Royal Society for Mentally Handicapped Children and Adults
MEP	Member of the European Parliament
MGOP	Memorandum of Good Practice (Home Office)
MH	Mental handicap
MH	Mental health
MHF	Mental Health Foundation
MHNA	Mental Handicap Nurses Association
MIND	National Association for Mental Health
MIRAS	Mortgage interest relief at source
MIS	Management Information System
MNDA	Motor Neurone Disease Association
MP	Member of Parliament
MP	Metropolitan Police
MRC	Medical Research Council
MS	Multiple Sclerosis
MSW	Medical Social Worker
NABC	National Association of Boys' Clubs
NACAB	National Association of Citizen's Advice Bureaux
NACRO	National Association for the Care and Resettlement of Offenders
NAI	Non-accidental injury
NAHT	National Association of Head Teachers
NALGO	National and Local Government Officers' Association
NAMCW	National Association for Maternal and Child Welfare
NAME	National Anti-racist Movement in Education

NANFC	National Association of Nursery and Family Care
NAOMI	National Association of Orientation and Mobility Instructors
NAPBH	National Association of Probation and Bail Hostels
NAPO	National Association of Probation Officers
NAPV	National Association for Prison Visitors
NARE	National Association for Remedial Education
NAS	National Autistic Society
NASCH	National Association of Swimming Clubs for the Handicapped
NASCT	National Association of Social Care Trainers
NASPO	National Association of Senior Probation Officers
NASWE	National Association of Social Workers in Education
NATCAT	National Association of Credit Accumulation and Transfer
NATFHE	National Association of Teachers in Further and Higher Education
NATOPSS	National Association of Training Officers in Personal Social Services
NAVB	National Association of Volunteer Bureaux
NAVHO	National Association of Voluntary Help Organisers
NAVSS	National Association of Victim Support Schemes
NAYPCAS	National Association of Young People's Counselling and Advice Services
NAYPIC	National Association of Young People in Care
NCASA	National Campaign Against Solvent Abuse
NCB	National Children's Bureau
NCC	National Consumer Council
NCG	National Council on Gambling
NCCL	National Council for Civil Liberties
NCET	National Council for Educational Technology
NCH	National Children's Homes
NCHA	National Care Home Owners Association
NCOPF	National Association for One Parent Families
NCSE	National Council for Special Education
NCSWD	National Council for Social Work with the Deaf
NCT	National Childbirth Trust
NCVO	National Council for Voluntary Organisations
NCVQ	National Council for Vocational Qualifications
NDCS	National Deaf Children's Society
NECUS	Homeless Network
NFCA	National Foster Care Association
NFHA	National Federation of Housing Associations
NFHC	National Federation of Housing Co-operatives
NH	Nursing Home
NHA	National Housewives Association
NHBC	National House-Building Council

NHI	National Health Insurance
NHR	National Housewives Register
NHS	National Health Service
NHSTA	National Health Service Training Authority
NI	National Insurance
NIACE	National Institute of Adult Continuing Education
NIACRO	Northern Ireland Association for Care and Resettlement of Offenders
NIAMH	Northern Ireland Association for Mental Health
NICD	Northern Ireland Council for Disability
NICHS	Northern Ireland Children's Holiday Scheme
NICVA	Northern Ireland Council for Voluntary Action
NIESR	National Institute of Economic and Social Research
NIPSA	Northern Ireland Public Service Alliance
NISW	National Institute for Social Work
NISWIS	National Institute for Social Work Information Service
NIVC	National Interactive Video Centre
NLP	Neurolinguistic Programming
NMGC	National Marriage Guidance Council
NNEB	National Nursery Examination Board
NOISE	National Organisation for Initiatives in Social Education
NORCAP	National Organisation for the Counselling of Adoptees and Parents
NPC	National Police Computer
NPFA	National Playing Fields Association
NSE	National Society for Epilepsy
NSF	National Schizophrenia Fellowship
NSPCC	National Society for Prevention of Cruelty to Children
NUPE	National Union of Public Employees
NUS	National Union of Students
NUT	National Union of Teachers
NVQ	National Vocational Qualification
NWPC	North Wales Practice Centre
NWR	National Women's Register
NYA	National Youth Agency
OD	Organisational Development
OD	Overdose
OFFER	Office of Electricity Regulation
OFGAS	Office of Gas Supply
OFSTED	Office for Standards in Education and Development
OFT	Office of Fair Trading
OFTEL	Office of Telecommunications

OFWAT	Office of Water Services
OHE	Office of Health Economics
OHP	Overhead projector
OL	Open learning
OPAS	Occupational Pensions Advisory Service
OPCS	Office of Population, Censuses and Surveys
OPF	One-parent family
OPH	Old People's Home
OPUS	Organisations for Parents under stress
OPWC	Old People's Welfare Committee
ORACLE	ITV & Channel 4's teletext service
OU	Open University
OUSA	Open University Students' Association
OXFAM	Oxford Committee of Famine Relief
PACE	Gay and lesbian project for advice counselling and education
PADE	Practice and Development Exchange (NISW)
PAGET	Paget Gorman Signed Speech
PAIN	Prisoners' Advice and Information Network
PAIN	Parents Against Injustice
PANN	Professional Association of Nursery Nurses
PARA	Plan for Active Retirement Association
PAS	Pregnancy Advisory Service .
PAT	Professional Association of Teachers
PAYE	Pay as you earn scheme
PC	Personal Computer
PCAS	Polytechnic Central Admissions System
PCSC	Preliminary Certificate in Social Care
PEP	Personal equity plan
PEP	Priority Estates Project
PEP	Political and Economic Planning
PER	Professional and Executive Recruitment
PES	Public Expenditure Survey
PGA	Prison Governors' Association
PGO	Principles of good organisation
PH	Physically handicapped
PHAB	Physically Handicapped and Able Bodied
PHCT	Primary Health Care Team
PICKUP	Professional Industrial and Commercial Updating
PLC	Practice Learning Centre
PLD	People with learning difficulties
PLWG	Plan work group
POA	Prison Officers' Association

PPA	Pre-School Playgroups Association
PPG	Programme provider groups
PPI	Placement provider initiative
PPIAS	Parent to Parent Information on Adoption Services
PQ	Post qualifying
PQ	Professional qualification
PQS	Post qualifying study programme
PROGRESS	The Disablement Income Group
PROP	Preservation of the Rights of Prisoners
PRT	Prison Reform Trust
PSA	Public Sector Agency
PSI	Policy Studies Institute
PSIGE	Psychologists Special Interest Group in the Elderly
PSR	Pre-sentence report
PSS	Personal Social Services
PSTC	Personal Services Training Committee
PSW	Principal Social Worker
PSW	Psychiatric Social Worker
PWS	Prisoners' Wives Service
QA	Quality Assurance
QR	Questionnaire review
QTP	Qualifying training policies
QUANGO	Quasi-Autonomous Non-Government Organisation
RA	Residents' association
RAC	Regional Advisory Council for Further Education
RADAR	Royal Association for Disability and Rehabilitation
RAP	Radical Alternatives to Prison
RAT	Racism awareness training
RCC	Rural Community Council
RCGP	Royal College of General Practitioners
RCN	Royal College of Nursing
RDDC	Residential, domiciliary and day care
REACH	Retired Executives Action Clearing House
RELATE	Formerly the Marriage Guidance Council
REMAP	Technical Aids for the Disabled (Scotland)
REMPLOY	Employment with Remploy
RGN	Registered General Nurse
RH	Rest/Residential Home
RHA	Regional Health Authority
RIBA	Royal Institute of British Architects
RICS	Royal Institute of Chartered Surveyors

RIPA	Royal Institute of Public Administration
RMN	Registered Mental Nurse
RNIB	Royal National Institute for the Blind
RNID	Royal National Institute for the Deaf
RNMH	Registered Nurse Mental Handicap (Scotland and Northern Ireland)
RNMS	Registered Nurse Mental Subnormality (England and Wales)
ROA	Rehabilitation of Offenders Act
RoSPA	Royal Society for the Prevention of Accidents
RPI	Retail Price Index
RSA	Royal Society of Arts
RSG	Rate Support Grant
RSH	Royal Society of Health
RSSPCC	Royal Scottish Society for Prevention of Cruelty to Children
RSVP	Retired and Senior Volunteer Programme
RTPI	Royal Town Planners Institute
SABEU	Scottish Adult Basic Education Unit
SACRO	Scottish Association for the Care and Resettlement of Offenders
SAMH	Scottish Association for Mental Health
SANDS	Stillbirth and Neonatal Death Society
SANE	Schizophrenia: A National Emergency
SASLI	Scottish Association for Sign Language Interpreters
SCA	Social Care Association
SCAFA	Scottish Child and Family Alliance
SCCO	Senior Child Care Officer
SCCL	Scottish Council for Civil Liberties
SCCVO	Scottish Council for Community and Voluntary Organisations
SCDC	Scottish Curriculum Development Committee
SCEC	Scottish Community Education Council
SCEMSC	Standing Conference of Ethnic Minority Senior Citizens
SCET	Scottish Council for Educational Technology
SCF	Save the Children (formerly Save the Children Fund)
SCHE	Scottish Council for Health Education
SCM	State Certified Midwife
SCODA	Standing Conference on Drug Abuse
SCOP	Society of Chief Officers of Probation
SCOPE	Scottish Pre-School Play Association
SCOSAC	Standing Committee of Sexually Abused Children
SCOTVEC	Scottish Vocational Education Council
SCOVO	Standing Conference for people with a mental handicap (Wales)
SCOYU	Standing Conference of Youth Organisation in Northern Ireland

SCRAC	Standing Conference of Regional Advisory Councils
SCSLG	Scottish Care Sector Liaison Group
SCVO	Scottish Council for Voluntary Organisations
SDA	Severe Disability Allowance
SED	Scottish Education Department
SEN	State enrolled nurse
SENNAC	Special Educational Needs National Advisory Council
SENSE	National Deaf-Blind and Rubella Association
SEQUAL	Special Equipment and Aids for Living
SER	Social Enquiry Report
SERPS	State earnings related pension scheme
SFI	Social Firms Initiative
SH	Scottish Homes – equivalent of Housing Corporation
SHAC	London Housing Aid Centre
SHARE	Selected Homes and Residential Environment
SHAW	Sheltered Housing and Workshops Project
SHEG	Scottish Health Education Group
SHELTER	National Campaign for the Homeless
SHHD	Scottish Home and Health Department
SIGA	Special Interest Group on Ageing
SIR	Social Inquiry Report
SKILL	National Bureau for Students with Disabilities
SLD	Severe learning difficulty
SMP	Statutory maternity pay
SNB	Board for Nursing, Midwifery and Health Visiting (Scotland)
SNNB	Scottish Nursery Nurses Board
SOVA	Society of Voluntary Associates
SPARKS	Sportsmen Pledged to Aid Research into Crippling
SPLASH	formerly Gingerbread holidays/one parent families
SPLL	Step parent Link Line
SPO	Senior Probation Officer
SPOD	Association to Aid the Sexual and Personal Relationships of People with a Disability
SPRING	Social Services Planning and Research Interest Group
SPS	Sheltered Placement Scheme
SPUC	Society for the Protection of the Unborn Child
SRCC	Social Science Research Council
SRHE	Society for Research into Higher Education
SRN	State Registered Nurse
SSA	Standard Spending Assessment
SSAC	Social Security Advisory Council
SSAFA	Soldiers', Sailors' and Airmen's Families Association

SSD	Social Services Department (England and Wales)
SSI	Social Services Inspectorate
SSMH	Scottish Society for Mentally Handicapped
SSP	Statutory sick pay
SSRG	Social Services Research Group
SSRIU	Social Services Research and Intelligence Unit
SSW	Senior Social Worker
STD	Seuxally transmitted disease
STOP	Society of Teachers Opposed to Physical Punishment
STUC	Scottish Trades Union Congress
SW	Social Work
SW	Social Worker
SWAS	Social Work Advisory Service
SWD	Social Work Department (Scotland)
SWE	Social Worker in Education
SWEA	Social Work Education Adviser (CCETSW)
SWET	Social Workers' Educational Trust
SWPC	South Wales Practice Centre
SWSG	Social Work Services Group (Scotland)
SWSO	Social Work Services Office
T and S	Travel and subsistence
TA	Transactional analysis
TACADE	Teachers Advisory Council on Alcohol and Drug Education
TAI CYMRU	Welsh equivalent of the Housing Corporation
TEC	Training and Enterprise Council
TEED	Training, Enterprise and Education Directorate
TESSA	Tax Exempt Special Savings Account MIRAS
TFW	Training for Work
TGWU	Transport and General Workers' Union
TIS	Travel to Interview Scheme
TMO	Tenant Management Organisation
TNAUK	Talking Newspaper Association of the UK
TP	Tenant participation
TPAS	Tenant Participation Advisory Service
TQM	Total Quality Management
TRIAL	Register of Independent Advisers Ltd
TSP	Training Support Panel
TT	Teetotal
TUC	Trades Union Congress
TVEI	Training and Vocational Education Initiative

UCAE	Universities' Council for Adult and Continuing Education
UCCA	Universities Central Council for Admissions
UFC	Universities Funding Council
UKCC	UK Central Council for Nursing, Midwifery and Health Visiting
UKCOSA	UK Council on Overseas Student Affairs
UKHCA	UK Homecare Association
UKIAS	UK Immigrants' Advisory Board
UN	United Nations
UNESCO	United Nations Educational, Scientific and Cultural Organisation
UNICEF	United Nations International Children's Emergency Fund
UP	Urban Programme
VA	Value Analysis
VA	Voluntary associate
VCS	Voluntary Community Service
VCT	Voluntary competitive tendering
VD	Venereal disease
VETG	Vocational Education and Training Group
VFM	Value for money
VOCAL	Voluntary Organisations Communication and Language
VOLCUF	Voluntary Organisations Liaison Council for Under Fives
VOPSS	Voluntary Organisations Personal Social Services Group
VPP	Voluntary Projects Programme
VR	Vocational Rehabilitation
VSO	Voluntary Services Overseas
WAB	Wales Advisory Board for Local Authority Higher Education
WAF	Women's Aid Federation
WATOPSS	Welsh Association of Training Officers in the Personal Social Services
WCC	World Council of Churches
WCVA	Wales Council for Voluntary Action
WEA	Workers' Educational Association
WHO	World Health Organisation
WHTSO	Welsh Health and Technical Services Organisation
WJEC	Welsh Joint Education Committee
WNB	Welsh National Board for Nursing, Midwifery and Health Visiting
WNCCC	Women's National Cancer Control Campaign
WO	Welsh Office
WPG	Work Planning Group
WRFE	Work Related Further Education
WRVS	Women's Royal Voluntary Service

YHA	Youth Hostels Association
YMCA	Young Men's Christian Association
YOI	Young Offender Institution
YT	Youth Training
YTP	Youth Training Programme (Northern Ireland)
YWCA	Young Women's Christian Association

Abortion

is the act of terminating a pregnancy before the foetus is developed enough to survive outside the mother's uterus. For social welfare workers, legislation through the 1967 Abortion Act, and amendments under the Human Fertilisation and Embryology Act 1990, provide the framework for their work. This frequently concerns linking pregnant women with medical practitioners, and pregnancy advisory and counselling services. NHS abortions are provided free in hospitals in cases legally approved under the legislation. Private abortions take place in private nursing homes and clinics. There is a twenty four week time limit to legal termination set by the existing legislation, which permits abortion on grounds of physical or mental health of the woman or her existing children.
c/f Family planning/Gillick

Acceptance

Care, affection, empathy, acceptance and understanding are among the fundamental elements of social welfare. Acceptance usually means recognising the 'worth' and positive aspects of an individual, that is, accepting the person for his or herself, free from value and moral judgements. This does not imply agreement with or condoning a client's behaviour or particular individual actions.
c/f Empathy/Non-directive

Accommodation

is a word with many different and specific meanings, depending upon the user group and context. Among them are: a) being flexible enough to allow another individual or group to join in or participate; b) specific types of residential or institutional provision; c) the individual ability to modify and adjust to changes in the personal environment; d) a change in visual perception, whereby the eye's lens can focus at different distances.

Accreditation of Prior Learning (APL)

The APL system is used in the National Vocational Qualifications scheme to award candidates with credits based on their prior learning and experience. The award of credits can be primarily based on the evidence supplied by a candidate in an APL portfolio, which consists of material such as a curriculum vitae; references and employer endorsements; examples of work performed and an indication of the skill level; certificates and qualifications.
c/f National Vocational Qualifications

Acting-out

is used in a number of ways. It is used, a) To describe training and therapeutic settings where individuals re-create situations which they have experienced in order to learn from their feelings and behaviour. This can include role-plays where participants act out roles. b) Freudian psychoanalysis uses the term to mean re-living a past experience, as a way of coming to terms with trauma. c) Acting-out is also used to describe individuals whose behaviour is creating a problem, and who are acting out their problems through anti-social behaviour, to attract attention.
c/f Role plays/Therapy

Action Learning

Put simply, action learning is supervised learning through doing. Social welfare trainers have been using action learning techniques for some years to assist staff and consumers to participate more fully in the learning process . . . learning on the job, particularly where it is carefully planned and supported, is a form of action learning. In training courses, the use of role play and case studies make learning more action-centred and less academic and removed from practice.
c/f Active listening/National Vocational Qualifications

Action Research

A commonly used model of social welfare research, where the researcher studies the working of an organisation or a social phenomenon and shares that research and any analysis with

Action Research (cont'd)

members of the organisation or activity. Sometimes the researcher will be an active part of the organisation or event, and this style of research is often utilised by researchers who are committed to the aim or purpose of the research, such as proving a need for more community facilities. Often such research is problem-centred and the findings are used to develop new strategies to alleviate the problem. A neat definition is 'research with an action outcome'.
c/f Evaluation and monitoring/Research

Action-Sets

are networks of organisations and individuals established to meet specific needs or achieve a goal. Utilising an action-set in social welfare implies a level of strategic planning. A self-help initiative such as the establishment of the *Big Issue* magazine which provides an income for its homeless street vendors is an example of a positive action-set. Social work staff may set up action-sets to create care management packages and individual care plans, which help to link the client or consumer with all the appropriate providers of services.
c/f Action learning/Case management/Networking

Active Listening

is a technique used by social care staff and counsellors to encourage individuals to feel more confident, uninhibited, and less shy or disadvantaged. It usually involves encouraging talk and reflection on feelings and events; questions and prompts, and paraphrasing and summary.
c/f Action learning

ACTs

ACTs is the popularly used acronym for the two Assessment and Counselling Teams which provide counselling and assessment support for people with disabilities. They primarily operate in areas not catered for by local employment rehabilitation centres or Asset centres (Assistance Towards Employment Centres).
c/f Assets/Employment rehabilitation centres/Employment rehabilitation centres

Adaptive Behaviour

covers a range of coping strategies and actions which enable the individual to survive and develop. In social welfare work, helping clients to adapt successfully to changes in circumstances is a major part of the social work task. For instance, vulnerable people often need assistance and support adapting to residential care or leaving residential care. The strengthening of adaptive behaviour is often critical to dealing positively with change.

c/f Learning disability/Vulnerable people

Addiction

A now unfashionable term to describe a person's 'dependence' upon a drug, activity or substance.

c/f Dependency

Admissibility

Evidence for consideration in court cases is collected usually in written form, but increasingly tape-recorded and video-recorded material is accepted as admissible in some proceedings. In wardship and care proceedings video-recordings are admissible, and since Judge Pigot reported, they are also admissible in child protection cases for potential criminal prosecution. The main problem in the test of admissibility is how far the aim of the recorders of such information is conveyed. Video recordings of children were intended to reduce the number of occasions they had to give evidence and reduce stress. However, the so-called Bexley experiment, 1988, confirmed doubts that the processes of investigation, prosecution and child protection could be combined in a single interview.

c/f Evidence

Admission

In social work, 'admission' usually means being admitted into residential care, either on a voluntary or compulsory basis. It is particularly used for patients admitted into hospital under the various section orders of the Mental Health Act 1983.

Admission is also used in the legal context for admitting guilt.

c/f Section 2, Section 3

Adolescence

is often used interchangeably with *youth* and *young people*. The onset of puberty is regarded as the beginning of adolescence, but its ending is less easy to define. Adolescence is essentially a period of experimentation and change. It can also be seen as a rehearsal for adulthood, during which young people try out different identities in preparation for adult life. Social welfare staff frequently have to deal with young people who are having difficulty with the transition and require understanding and patience to help them cope with adult rights and responsibilities.

c/f Youth social work/Youth work

Adoption

is a highly complex area. Social work staff employed by local authorities, staff of an approved adoptive society or parents and guardians can apply for an adoptive order. The reasons for adoption are the irrevocable break-up of a family, or the permanent inability of parents to care and support their child(ren). The effect of adoption is to transfer responsibility for a child to new parents. The Adoption Act 1976 and the Children Act 1989 govern matters relating to adoption.

Most adoption agencies including local authorities use forms and guidance provided by the British Agencies for Adoption and Fostering (BAAF). Adoption proceedings go through two steps. Firstly, an internal process involves an adoption panel assessing the interests of the child, assessing existing parenting arrangements and considering prospective adoptive parents. The second step is a hearing in a magistrate's or High Court. In this process, a child needs to be 'freed' for adoption, then an adoption order can be made. If natural parents do not give their consent for adoption, consent can be dispensed with if the court believes that the parent or guardian a) cannot be found or is incapable of giving consent, b) is withholding agreement unreasonably; c) has failed persistently in discharging parental responsibility; d) has abandoned or neglected the child; e) has persistently ill-treated the child; f) has seriously ill-treated the child.

Adoption is a final step and great care needs to be taken to assess the need for the action and the appropriateness of adopters.

c/f British Agencies for Adoption and Fostering/Family placement/ Foster care

Adult Literacy/Numeracy

initiatives are run both by local education authorities and voluntary agencies. Substantial numbers of children leaving school still cannot deal with everyday literacy or numeracy tasks such as filling in forms, checking pay slips and using a phone directory. Organisations such as the Workers' Educational Association run local courses, as do local further education colleges and open learning centres. Since 1980, the Adult Literacy and Basic Skills Unit (ALBSU) has provided information and advice for establishing adult literacy, numeracy and basic skills courses.
c/f Social skills

Adult Training Centres

c/f Social Education Centres

Advocacy

is a social work method frequently employed by community-based social work staff. There is a danger of paternalism inherent in advocacy, and social workers are advised to act only on behalf of, or represent the views of others, where this is a) genuinely in the best interest of the service user, and b) it does not create an over-dependence upon the advocate. Empowerment requires the social welfare worker to 'advocate', consult and reflect as one single process. In the USA, advocacy is seen as a basic obligation of the social worker. In Britain, advocacy is seen more as one of many social work tools. Advocacy schemes have also been developed to enable the views of, for instance, people with learning difficulties, elderly, mentally confused and frail people to be appropriately represented.
c/f Empowerment

Affiliation Order

This order is made if the court decides that a man against whom an order has been made is the father of a particular baby. The court can order the man to make regular contributions towards the maintenance of the child.
c/f Magistrates court/Maintenance Order

Affirmative Action

is action designed to reverse the effects of discrimination and prejudice. Also known as positive discrimination, affirmative action programmes are used to offer extra support for individuals and groups such as disabled people, ethnic minorities, the unemployed and ex-offenders. Many social workers spend a good deal of their time assisting disadvantaged people with organising community action activities.

c/f Discrimination

Affordability

is used in housing services to describe the system of subsidies and benefits which the State provides to offer adequate housing at an affordable price. Inducements to buy housing and become home owners or owner occupiers have run in parallel with legislation under the 1988 and 1989 Housing Acts to increase rent levels in the social housing market.

Housing Benefit is used as an income supplement designed to make accommodation affordable, but many low income families fall into what has been called the *affordability* gap which makes it very difficult to pay for housing and pay for other necessities.

Local authorities dealing with planning applications are increasingly encouraging developers to include a proportion of affordable accommodation in any new-build schemes, based on assessed local housing need.

Affordability is also sometimes used in other welfare contexts to mean more generally that a particular service makes good use of available resources and is, therefore, affordable.

c/f Housing benefit/Social housing

After-care

describes services provided through social work, health and offenders' work and includes provision offered either voluntarily or compulsorily to individuals on leaving some form of residential care. Hospitals, prisons, children's homes and so on all have after-care services; the official title of the Probation Service is the Probation and After Care Service.

After-care (cont'd)

Support for many people who have left residential settings
(for example for mentally or physically ill), under voluntary or
compulsory care and supervision orders, is frequently inappropriate
or inadequate. Community Care should provide more integration of
services and enable consumers to become partners in determining
the services required. The creation of various forms of support
networks is an important aspect of aftercare.
c/f Community Care/Leaving care/Probation

After-school Clubs

c/f Out-of-school clubs

Ageism

is used to describe individual or institutional forms of discrimination
against older people. Stereotyping older people as being less able is
a form of ageism.
c/f Discrimination/Sexism

Agency

is used as a synonym for *organisation*, whether it is a statutory
or voluntary organisation. In the 1990s, agencies in social care
frequently act as purchasers of services and providers of services for
a range of consumers.
c/f Multi-agency/Statutory services/Voluntary agency

Agents of Social Control

are institutions and agencies such as the police, education and social
work, which are charged with upholding the prevailing values of the
society in which they operate. Used pejoratively, the term is applied
to agencies and their staff which are oppressive and act to restrict
freedom. Conversely, they can be seen as a necessary influence to
maintain order and balance in society.
c/f Social control

AIDs [Acquired Immune Deficiency Syndrome]

Social welfare staff have become increasingly involved in multi-disciplinary work with AIDs carriers. Counselling, clinics, therapy and special residential units are among the facilities in which social work staff and others may work with people who have contracted the AIDs virus. The virus is contracted through exchange of the body's fluids such as blood or semen. Early cases were predominently amongst individuals who had engaged in drug use involving needles, and homosexual and bi-sexual males. The incubation period of the virus is five years or more and this makes estimating the current number of AIDs carriers extremely difficult, but increasingly women and children and heterosexual males are being found to be infected.
c/f HIV/Sexually transmitted diseases

'Alarm Call' System

is provided by many local authorities, using British Telecom lines, along with *pagers*. These provide elderly people with a communications system which links them together, and provides emergency back-up.
c/f Community-based services for elderly people

Alcohol Abuse/Misuse

Alcoholism, alcohol dependency and alcohol abuse are synonymous terms for the condition where the consumption of alcohol starts to physically or mentally impair the abuser. Over-indulgence can lead to physical assaults on other people and damage to property. Statutory and voluntary social welfare time may be spent dealing with the consequences of alcohol misuse – rifts in relationships, unemployment, ill health, physical and mental impairment and injury. Common social welfare responses to help people with alcohol related problems are counselling, therapeutic programmes and residential services.
c/f Counselling/Dependency/Therapy

Alienation

is used loosely to describe almost any circumstances where individuals or groups of people feel disenfranchised, ostracised and

Alienation (cont'd)

separate from other people or the society in which they are living. Hegel originated the use of 'alienation', and Marx extended the concept as a precursor of working class revolution. The concept was also made popular by the American sociologist, Merton, to describe the situation of disadvantaged people, particularly the young, who turned to crime and other deviant acts in response to their felt lack of opportunities to achieve conventional social success and status.
c/f Anomie

Allocation

In social work, this usually refers to how, and to whom, cases are distributed after referral. Confusingly, the word is also used to describe resource allocation. In housing, allocations of accommodation are a major function of housing authorities and housing associations. In housing, social welfare and health, resource allocation must often be prioritised, according to social need, policies, procedures and so on. In social work, child protection is always given high priority. In housing, points are allocated to special needs groups, such as single parents with small children, who will have priority in the 'points system' over single people without responsibilities.
c/f Case/Casework/Points system/Referral

Almshouses

These are houses and other accommodation provided by charitable trusts for the elderly. The name is historically based on the idea of philanthropic 'alms' given for relief of the poor and destitute. The trustees who now administer the remaining almshouses do so on the basis of very local admissions policies. There are over 26,000 almshouse units most of which are loosely co-ordinated through the Almshouses Association.
c/f Sheltered housing

Ancillary Staff

are any staff members who are not directly involved in the core task. For instance, in a social work office, the caretaker and cleaners

Ancillary Staff (cont'd)

are often referred to as ancillary staff, as are non-qualified or non-teaching staff in schools.

Animateurs/Animation

In the 1970s and 1980s, the group leader or facilitator was often called the 'Animateur', which literally means the 'organiser of a lively activity'. The process of *animation* was seen as an active one of encouraging participation. In the 1990s, group leaders in social welfare are more concerned with empowerment and partnership working and so the terms *facilitators* and *enablers* for staff who work with groups are more fashionable.
c/f Enabler/Facilitators/Groupwork

Anomie

is a condition first described by Durkheim, but now often used by social welfare commentators to explain the condition of socially and economically disadvantaged people. Being in a state of anomie is to be powerless, rootless and without personal goals. It is related to *alienation*, but whilst alienation suggests positive rejection of social values and beliefs, anomie is about giving up and despair.
c/f Alienation

Anti-social

is an imprecise and potentially stigmatising term which refers to individuals or forms of behaviour which are causing distress or conflict for other members of a community or society in general. Where offending occurs, anti-social behaviour is regarded as needing extra social intervention, such as behaviour modification programmes to change that behaviour pattern.
c/f Behaviour modification/Labelling

Appraisal

An appraisal is used when an assessment of a situation or more normally a person is required. This term is used to describe both the assessment of client needs, and as a specific technique to evaluate the current performance of staff members. The person conducting an

Appraisal (cont'd)

appraisal is known as an appraiser. Under the NVQ system, appraisal is known as assessment of competence, undertaken by recognised, trained assessors.
c/f Assessment/National Vocational Qualifications

Area Team

The area team is the most common unit of organisation for local authority social work staff. An area team of social work staff may assess and provide all the services for a defined geographical area, which may also be seen locally as a distinct community. These generic services may also require supplementary services of a specialist kind to meet the special needs of the individual for residential assistance or specialist skills.
c/f Generic/Social work/Specialist

Assertiveness

Assertiveness training and techniques are used to encourage effective communication, particularly in work with women and disadvantaged groups. Assertiveness is different from aggression in social welfare circles; it is seen as a desirable goal, encouraging individuals to voice their views in a variety of settings such as discussion groups, work teams and meetings.
c/f Empowerment/Self-actualisation/Self-awareness

Assessment

This is a major component of social work practice, requiring evaluation of the most appropriate course of action (or diversion/ inaction) for each individual and group being worked with. Assessment implies observation, information gathering and appraisal, professional decision-taking and action. It is usual for individual meetings with clients and behaviour and performance in groups to be used as the basis for assessment. The assessment will be recorded in writing and may form the basis for an individual care plan or referral. Increasingly, 'consumers' are invited to share in the assessment process, form their own judgements on, and make contributions to the 'outcome'.

Assessment

Assessment is also important in staff training to evaluate their competence. Assessors are increasingly used to monitor staff – performance, as measured against agreed standards laid down by the professional bodies through course requirements, National Vocational Qualifications, and similar systems of skill assessment.
c/f Child Assessment Order/Monitoring and evaluation/National Vocational Qualifications/Recording

Asset Centres

There are currently six 'Assistance Towards Employment Centres' (ASSETs) nationally as part of the special rehabilitation services provided through the Employment Service. They are run in office-type premises and provide assessment facilities for people with disabilities.
c/f ACTs/Employment rehabilitation service

Assured Tenancy

is a contract for tenants of housing associations and private landlords. It came into effect following the 1988 Housing Act.

Asylum

Asylum means a place of refuge. The need for this has not gone away, though the term asylum has largely pejorative overtones related to the public image of large scale psychiatric hospitals.
In mental health work, the implementation of the National Health Service and Community Care Act 1990 represents a major challenge. Replacing institutional care with community-based care and support requires careful planning to ensure that 24-hour cover for users still exists. In this sense, asylum means a place of refuge – the need for which has not gone away.
c/f Institutions/Mental health/Residential care

'At Risk'

Vulnerable people, including homeless, older and disabled people and those who may offend, are frequently referred to as being at risk. Social welfare programmes are sometimes targeted at

'At Risk' (cont'd)

communities because social conditions are thought to put the well-being of the community members at risk. Similarly, preventative programmes designed to reduce delinquency have often taken 'at risk' populations of people, such as first time juvenile offenders, and provided activities, group work and counselling to try and divert further offending behaviour. 'Risk' assessments are frequently made as part of an overall assessment process.

c/f Vulnerable people

Atonement

c/f Mediation/Reparation

Attendance Allowance (AA)

This state benefit is paid to individuals who need looking after because of illness or disability. The amount granted depends upon the level of supervision required. The allowance is available to anyone over two years of age. The Social Security Act 1975 and the Social Security (Attendance Allowance) Regulations 1983 regulate the payment and eligibility for AA.

Attitudinal Testing

These are special types of test usually presented in the form of a questionnaire. They are used in assessment of individual attitudes and predispositions to types of behaviour. Measurement in attitudinal tests is by means of rating scales, for instance if '1' is 'agree completely' and '5' means 'totally disagree', which number 1, 2, 3, 4, 5, represents your response to the question?

Careers service staff, personnel officers and trainers involved in 'unblocking' staff teams and management, use this type of test to assess the suitability of people for particular types of task. Most attitude tests produce results which have to be *coded* into sets of responses, dealing with different types of *attitude* or *preference*.

c/f Assessment/Questionnaire/Rating scales

Audit

An audit is an activity which systematically assesses current systems and practices, and proposes ways of ensuring minimum acceptable standards and achieving improvements. The audit process usually investigates objectives, measurable standards of performance and organisational structures. It then offers ways of developing and improving core values, attaining standards, and monitoring within a quality assurance context.

The concept of a social audit (as opposed to a purely financial audit) has been developed to improve care and has been most thoroughly developed in the NHS. The principal aims of this type of audit have been to: improve consistency of care; improve the quality of service delivery; encourage the measurement and monitoring of practice; allow 'best practice' standards to be developed; improve cost-efficiency and obtain value-for-money.
c/f Quality assurance/Value for money

Autism

is a severe developmental disorder which is characterised by a failure to relate to the external world of people and objects. Deficient or abnormal patterns of communication, various forms of compulsive and repetitive behaviour, and withdrawal are further symptoms. People with autism present great difficulties for their parents, care staff and other adults sharing their care. Special educational and residential facilities are available for some autistic people.

B

Befriending

is a method of linking people in need with a 'friend' in the community
or residential home. The befriender is usually a volunteer and offers
support and attention on a non-compulsory basis. Befriending
schemes are often co-ordinated by social services departments or
local voluntary agencies as a means of helping people in need. They
can assist a variety of client groups including young people in trouble
or at risk, older people and people with mental health problems.

Behaviour Modification

This is a psychological method for changing behaviour; requiring
identification of behaviour, and possibly attitudes which are causing
problems; assessment; specification of modification[s] required, and
adoption of a programme to bring about change. It is most often
used with offenders, and behaviour modification programmes often
rely on a carrot and stick approach of reinforcement of positive
attitudes and behaviour, and negative reinforcement and punishment
of problem behaviour.

Social work staff have sometimes resisted the technique because
it can be seen as pathologising and personalising an individual as
deviant or criminal. However, many offender programmes are based
on interventions aimed at conditioning and changing behaviour and
making individuals much more conscious about the effects of their
behaviour – thus owning their own problem.

c/f Conditioning/Experiential learning/Pathologise/Psychology

Benefits

cover the entitlement to state payments in respect of a particular
condition, such as pregnancy, sickness, unemployment or low
income. Some benefits are means tested, others relate to payment
of national insurance contributions. Welfare Rights work is primarily
concerned with encouraging people to take-up their benefit

Benefits (cont'd)

entitlements. Benefits also include the right to free provisions and services such as housing, medicine and dental care.
c/f Family credit/Means testing/Take-up/Welfare rights

Bereavement

Making sense of loss and adjusting to that loss involves both psychological and social pressure. Many paid and unpaid social welfare staff working in residential and community settings find themselves developing supportive relationships with people who are grieving. This can help individuals to cope more successfully with grief, to understand their own emotional responses, and re-build their lives.

Bereavement counselling takes place in a variety of settings and contexts. Among them are: cot-deaths; death of partners and close relatives; in the aftermath of tragedies such as Hillsborough and King's Cross.
c/f Counselling/Loss

Bibliotherapy

is a specific technique utilising literature – novels, poems and diary writings, to help individuals find words to express their own feelings. It is used in bereavement and loss situations where individuals are encouraged to read as a way of exploring and resolving their own feelings and difficulties. It can also be used in group work settings, with the counsellor reading a poem or extract to the group and then asking for a variety of responses.
c/f Bereavement/Counselling/Groupwork/Loss

Biofeedback

A controversial self-treatment that is sometimes used in therapeutic programmes. It enables people to use mechanical and electronic instrumentation to monitor their body, heart rate, brain-waves, muscle tension. Individuals can learn to control these physiological processes, which are 'fed back' as results, even though they may not be able to explain how they have achieved the results.
c/f Therapy

Blind and Partially Sighted People

Under the Disabled Persons act 1986, and other legislation, blind and partially sighted people are entitled to the whole range of services available for physically disabled people. The social services department must compile a register of all blind and partially sighted people in their area, but registration is voluntary. The definition of blindness is 'so blind as to be unable to perform any work for which eyesight is essential'. Mobility Officers and Rehabilitation Officers are employed by some authorities to offer help with outdoor and indoor mobility, braille, and reading and writing. There are many voluntary organisations working with visually impaired people and the Royal National Institute for the Blind (RNIB) is a major source of information and advice.

c/f Sensory impairments

Boundaries/Boundary Maintenance

This concept has been developed into a practical way of client empowerment and sharing and caring in a protected environment for groupwork clients. In its simplest form, a group will determine the agreed boundary rules for the group members. It is then the group facilitator's task to ensure, hopefully with the agreement and co-operation of the group, that the boundary is maintained.

In a different context, 'boundaries' are developed as a management method to ensure that work is kept within agreed limits (boundaries), which may be financial; geographical; to do with types of client or methods and locations for contact work; time and general areas of responsibility.

c/f Contracts/Groupwork/Safeguards

Bound-over

The 1991 Criminal Justice Act extended the use of binding-over to the parents and guardians of juveniles and children. This is a further application of the approach of the Children Act 1989 which started to define the range of parental responsibilities. Parents can be bound over to exercise proper control over their charges for a specified period of time.

Binding over also occurs in common law proceedings, where the court binds over a person for an amount of money and period of

Bound-over (cont'd)

time. Further offending leads to forfeit of the agreed bond. Witnesses in court can be bound over to keep the peace.
c/f Parental responsibility/Recognisance

Brainstorming

This is a group technique which involves a facilitator inviting very quick, off-the-top-of-the-head responses from members of a staff team, trainees or clients. The responses and ideas may be on any subject or problem, the aim being to promote creativity. The facilitator writes up *all* the ideas offered on a flip chart or blackboard for later analysis and discussion. Brainstorming is a useful method of stimulating ideas and group interaction, and is a group problem-solving technique.
c/f Groupwork/Active listening

Breach Proceedings

occur when ex-offenders fail to meet the conditions of their post-release supervision by the Probation Service. Prisoners released on licence are expected to keep contact with their probation officer and not re-offend. Breaking these conditions may lead to breach proceedings which are heard in a magistrate's court and can result in up to £1,000 fine and return to prison.
c/f Licensees/Probation and after-care service

Brief Treatment/Therapy

A term describing any social welfare intervention which is intentionally time-limited, or limited by a fixed number of meetings or course of treatment. Brief treatment can be contracted with a client and tends to be focussed on a specific goal or problem. The term is also sometimes applied to contact with a client which ends quickly in an unplanned way.
c/f Behaviour modification/Contracts

British Agencies for Adoption and Fostering

is an association of agencies promoting good advice in adoption fostering and social work with children and families. Their guidance,

British Agencies for Adoption and Fostering (cont'd)

information and model forms are used by many local authorities and adoption agencies.

c/f Adoption/Family placement/Foster care

British Standard 5750 (BS 5750/ISO 9000)

BS 5750/ISO 9000 are the British and international standards for quality management, which are increasingly being applied to care and health organisations. Although designed originally for use in the manufacturing and commercial sectors, BS 5750 contains principles and procedures which can provide a quality framework for developing and evaluating social care services.

Briefly, BS 5750 defines a quality system as: find out and assess user or customer needs; develop services and facilities which will meet those needs; monitor the services and rectify problems as they occur. The procedures have been applied in the health services and increasingly in the residential services, as a way of generating 'quality' in meeting contract specification requirements.

c/f Quality assurance/Total quality management

Buzz or Cluster Group

These are a small group technique for between three and eight participants, used as a means of promoting participation and for stimulating ideas. A facilitator sets a particular task, problem or subject. The group may be asked to report back the main points to the larger group, within a relatively short time-scale, usually no longer than one hour. They work fast, hence the notion of 'buzzing' with ideas, and may utilise the brainstorming system of generating creative contributions from participants.

c/f Brainstorming/Groupwork/Workshops

C

Care

is used in various senses. It is used to describe the whole system of welfare, encompassing staff employed by local authorities, voluntary agencies, private agencies and voluntary and self-help. This 'care' system employs staff often called care staff or simply carers, who work in domiciliary and community care settings; and in a range of residential establishments. Any child in England and Wales can also be subject to a *Care Order* up to the age of seventeen. The Children Act 1989, under Section IV, contains the provisions for care and supervision of young people and the grounds on which a young person or child may be referred into *compulsory care*. Being *in care* is usually used to describe the range of residential alternatives to living at home, both on a compulsory and voluntary basis.
c/f Care Order/Community Care/Domiciliary care/In care/Residential care/Social care

Care Management

Care management and case management are frequently used interchangeably. However, following the Griffiths Report, published in 1988 there was pressure to use care management and care manager as the most appropriate terms to describe the task of social workers in assessing and tailoring care packages to meet clients' needs. Subsequently, the NHS and Community Care Act (1990) in section 47 defined the term as the assessment and care planning which local authorities must introduce for managing the needs of individuals and their carers. Case management is then usually used to describe a part of the care management task.
c/f Case management

Care Order

A care order is granted by a court, usually a magistrate's court. Applications for the making of a care order can be made by a local authority or the NSPCC. The proceedings follow the requirements of

Care Order (cont'd)

the Children Act 1989 and should involve the applicant; the child and often their guardian ad litem; everyone with parental responsibility for the child and any other natural parents, and persons who are caring for the child at the time proceedings are commenced.

Under section 31(2) of the Children Act the main reasons for court making a care order are that:
a) the child concerned is suffering, or is likely to suffer significant harm; *and* b) that the harm, or likelihood of harm, is attributable to (i) the care given to the child, or likely to be given to him/her if the order were not made, not being what it would be reasonable to expect a parent to give him/her; or (ii) the child's being beyond parental control.

The court requires that the local authority provides a plan of detailed proposals for the care order. Contact with parents under the order is an important feature. All parties are invited to comment on the plan (under section 34 of the Act). A care order is a compulsory measure of care and is designed to provide the best conditions for the welfare of the child in accommodation chosen by the social services department of the local authority.
c/f Care/Child abuse/Child sexual abuse/Guardian ad litem/ Residential care

Care Sector Consortium

The National Vocational Qualifications for health and social care are co-ordinated through the national lead body, the Care Sector Consortium. This is a mixed group of representatives from public and private employers, trade unions and professional associations. The Consortium was established in 1988 and its major tasks are to establish and monitor standards of competence in health and social care. It is planned to eventually replace the Consortium with a new body called the Occupational Standards Council.
c/f Competence/National Vocational Qualifications

Case

From the moment a social worker starts to keep a record about an individual's needs, that person is usually referred to as a 'case'. The

Case

procedures for effectively organising a case are called casework, and the management of cases is case management.

c/f Case management/Casework

Case Conference

This is a forum for discussion and decision-taking about needs in a particular case situation. The format of case conferences varies between different agencies. Usually, all the professional agencies involved in a case will send a representative to the case conference meeting. Parents, the client, relatives and friends may be asked to provide information for consideration; increasingly the client is invited to attend and to contribute.

Case conferences may take place throughout a client's career, but particularly at the beginning when various interventions are being considered. Subsequently, case conferences will review the effectiveness of an intervention, for example, the operation of a Care Order, and decide further action on this basis.

c/f Case/Case review/Casework

Case File

Case files are the main form of record-keeping used by social welfare staff. Sometimes criticised for subjectivity, they are the most important collection of documents relating to an individual or a family, and their problem and social circumstances. Where the background of the case is provided in some detail, this file is often called the *case history*. Case files will contain a growing number of notes and assessment reports as time goes by. For this reason, it is increasingly viewed as good practice to transfer the most important information on to data captive sheets which can be held and analysed through a computer system. The question of open access for clients to case files is increasingly under discussion, as is the wider question of confidentiality and the storing of personal information.

c/f Casework/Data capture sheets/Personal information

Case History

c/f Case file

Case Load

The number of cases for which an individual worker, team or organisation has responsibility is known as the caseload. Different types of case require very different levels of time and intervention. There is also a question mark regarding when contact with a person using a social welfare service constitutes a 'case'.

The management of caseloads is both an individual and team task, both in terms of the size of caseloads, but also in terms of how cases are allocated and what interventions are recommended.
c/f Case/Case file/Casework

Case Management

Case management is the targeting of resources effectively through proper referral and assessment procedures; planning and delivery of care; monitoring delivery of services and reviewing client needs. The concept of case management has been introduced principally through the 'Care in the Community' legislation. The case manager has the overall responsibility for the creation of a suitable package of services, designed to provide a quality of service, and value for money to the client or consumer. A case manager should hold budgetary responsibility in order to achieve service efficiency and cost effectiveness, usually now defined within a quality assurance framework.
c/f Care management/Caseload/Casework/Community Care/Griffiths/ Quality assurance

Case Review

This is the formal review of a social work, health or housing 'case'. It should provide the opportunity for all professionals involved in a case to evaluate, or re-evaluate the provision(s) being made and consider alternative actions. *Case conferences*, where all those involved in a case actually meet to discuss present and future options, are part of the case planning and assessment review process.

Case reviews contribute to the monitoring and evaluation of the quality, effectiveness and cost of services.
c/f Case conference/Evaluation

Case Study

This is a method of providing a written record which produces information on a particular individual, group, family, community or intervention. A case study can never be entirely objective, but it can provide material for evaluation and as a training aid. For instance, a case study of a child abuse case will provide lessons which can inform future interventions.
c/f Evaluation

Casework

Casework is the most traditional method of social work. It involves a series of processes: referral; assessment; goal setting and intervention planning; action; review and evaluation. The same individual worker(s) may not be involved throughout, and assessment, in particular, is frequently undertaken by a different worker (or section). The assessment stage of casework is completed through interviews, observation, and general information collection.

During the process of casework, increasing emphasis is placed on trying to help the consumer or client have choices and become *empowered* to work out their own solutions. It also seeks to use a variety of community facilities, and informal as well as formal networks of support – such as families, friends, neighbours, to achieve its purpose.

Casework involves both *direct* assistance (for instance, counselling, advice and information giving), and *indirect* (for instance, advocacy) means of influencing the changes required to improve a client's circumstances and situation.
c/f Case management/Consumer/Empowerment

Caution

Formal cautions can be used by police inspectors in cases where a person admits guilt to an offence, but where the police feel that the case is very trivial or where the person has no previous record of convictions. Social services, probation and the Crown Prosecution staff may all be consulted concerning whether or not to proceed with a prosecution. In nearly a third of indictable cases cautions are used (based on 1990 Home Office cases). Young people and

Caution (cont'd)

children are more likely to receive cautions from police officers than adults.
c/f Crown Prosecution Service/Police

Child Abuse

is a rather loose term which is normally used to describe all forms of neglect, physical injury, sexual abuse and emotional abuse which can constitute significant harm for a child. These four categories come from the Department of Health publication *Working Together*, first issued in 1988. They are not quite the same as the definition of significant harm used in Section 31 of the Children Act 1989, but together they provide the basis for applying for a care order.
c/f Care Order/Child Sexual Abuse

Child Assessment Order (CAS)

The Child Assessment Order (CAS) is a specific order which can be made by a court after an application by the NSPCC or a local authority. It is intended, under the Children Act 1989, to be used in cases where there is *suspicion* that a child may suffer or has suffered significant harm and that an assessment of the child's health and treatment is required. It is the lesser order, compared to the Emergency Protection Order, and is aimed at plugging a gap between cases which are 'emergencies' because harm is believed to be apparent, and no action, investigation or assessment taking place. It is a short term child protection response and the assessment must be completed within seven days. A child *may* be separated from their family in order for the assessment to take place.
c/f Assessment/Care Order/Emergency Protection Order/Supervision Order

Child Benefit (CB)

was established under the Child Benefit Act in 1975. It is universally available to the adult responsible for a child under sixteen (or nineteen in full time secondary education). Child benefit is not means tested and is non-contributory.
c/f Family credit/Income support

Child Care

Between 1948 and 1971, child care services were provided by local
authorities through specialist Children's Departments. Since then
there have been a wider variety of services provided for children
under headings such as specialist education; intermediate treatment;
assessment; residential or community care; adoption and fostering;
probation and education welfare.

Child care is used to describe systems of service delivery.
Increasingly, these services do not 'belong' to the local authority
Social Services department, but are the responsibility of both
statutory and voluntary agencies including Health, Education,
Housing, NSPCC, Save the Children, Barnardos, National Children's
Homes, and so on.
c/f Care/Child protection/Children's rights/In care/Social care

Child-Centred

The approach known as child-centred work focusses on social
work as a means of intervening in the best interests of the child.
It takes account of, at all times, the wishes and feelings of that
child. At times, the approach can bring staff into conflict with other
professionals and parents.
c/f Client-centred

Child Guidance

is a service provided through the local education authority. Principally
it deals with children who are thought to have educational, emotional
or behavioural problems. Referrals are made from schools and health
practitioners. The service is multi-disciplinary with the majority of
staff being educational psychologists, although social workers are
also employed as members of the child guidance team. The services
of a child psychiatrist are also generally available.

Child Minders

have to be registered with the local authority social services
department and receive payment for the care they provide. Child-
minding describes the activity of looking after children on behalf of

Child Minders (cont'd)

parents or guardians in any non-residential setting. Child minders are particularly used by single parents and parents whose patterns of work makes statutory (or extended family) child care impracticable. Registration and inspection of child minders and premises offering this service have traditionally been somewhat patchy and erratic, but are meant to apply to all child minders offering care more than two hours per day for children of eight years and under. Nannies working in their employers' homes are not subject to this inspection and registration procedure.

c/f Creche/Nursery/Play group

Child Protection

Child Protection is the umbrella term used to describe the work of statutory and voluntary agencies in protecting children and young people from harm and abuse. Some of the work is regarded as preventative, through educating adults and young people themselves about the risks which exist in society. Other work involves specialist counselling and investigation of suspected abuse, and interviewing both perpetrators and victims of abuse. The specialist interview of children who have been abused is normally called a *disclosure*.

The Convention on the Rights of the Child issued in 1989 by the United States embodies a detailed set of standards for the defence of children against neglect and abuse, worldwide. In the UK, the child's right to protection and the power for authorities to intervene in families is established under the NSPCC inspired 1933 Children and Young Persons Act and a succession of legislation leading to the 1989 Children Act.

c/f Child care/Child sexual abuse/Children's rights/Disclosure

Child Protection Registers

The registers reflect professional judgements regarding the future risk to children of significant harm or injury. As many as two-thirds of cases of child abuse are not substantiated and drop out before registration occurs. In 1992 the DOH reported that 0.62 per thousand children were registered. The operation of child protection registers is a non-statutory operation, and strangely they are *not* governed

Child Protection Registers

by legislation. This makes the practical operation of care under proceedings more confusing since the four categories of child abuse for registration: neglect, physical injury, sexual abuse and emotional abuse, do not tie in precisely to the legal definition of significant harm.
c/f Care Order/Child protection/Child sexual abuse

Child Protection Teams

In both local authority social services departments and in the NSPCC, specialist child protection teams have been established to co-ordinate official responses to child abuse. The aim of these teams is to provide the most effective support for children who have been abused, or who are suspected of being at risk of abuse. Team members usually work very closely together, but have different professional expertise. Typically, members may include staff with backgrounds in social work; psychology; education; health and psychotherapy.
c/f Multi-agency/Multi-disciplinary

Child Sexual Abuse

The law does not define child abuse or child sexual abuse, but there are a list of offences which relate to actions of a cruel and indecent nature. Child sexual abuse or CSA as it is often referred to, is the general term used in the media and amongst most social welfare staff to describe a range of injurious actions effected on children. The charges of importuning and indecent assault are frequently used in such cases by the Crown Prosecution Service.

The work of social welfare staff in cases of suspected child sexual abuse involves multi-agency collaboration, particularly between social services, psychologists, police and doctors. Most social services departments and NSPCC offices have their own specialist child protection teams.

A sequence of well publicised child abuse cases including Cleveland, Rochdale and the Orkneys have led to substantial changes in the way social workers conduct investigations. These led to the establishment of the Home Office Advisory Group which

Child Sexual Abuse (cont'd)

drafted the Memorandum of Good Practice for Interviewing Children
(Home Office 1992).
c/f Child abuse/Child protection/Child protection teams

Child Support Agency (CSA)

Following from the Child Support Act 1991, this new agency has
been established to take over most of the courts' functions in
determining payments for children after matrimonial proceedings.
Staff of the CSA are also responsible for enforcement of maintenance
payments which can include deductions from wages or income
support and inspection of tax and benefit information.
c/f Conciliation/Divorce

Children 'In Need'

The provision of appropriate services for children 'in need' are a
major part of the work of local authorities and a growing number of
voluntary agencies. The definition of children in need is taken from
the Children Act 1989 as: failing to develop or achieve a reasonable
standard of health and general development (physical, mental,
intellectual, emotional, social and behavioural) and disabled children.
   Services can be directly offered to children or parents and families
of the child.
c/f Child protection

Children's Hearings

In Scotland, the 1968 Social Work (Scotland) Act established
Children's Hearings as an alternative to the Juvenile Court. The
Hearing is unlike a court, and the procedure is run by a *Children's
Panel* advised by an executive officer called a Reporter. Any child
who may need compulsory measures of care is referred to the
Reporter, who can either taken no action or call a Hearing. At a
Hearing, two panel members and a panel chairperson (who are
lay-people) listen to the views of the child, parents, the child's
representative, social workers and education staff and decide what
course of action to take in the best interests of the child. A child may
be referred for residential or non-residential supervision or

Children's Hearings

be discharged. What is so different at a Children's Hearing is the involvement of families and the child in a process which is far less formal and non-adversarial. Approximately 50 per cent of referrals to the Reporter are sent to a Hearing.
c/f Children's Panel/Reporter

Children's Homes

are homes run by local authorities, voluntary and private organisations, providing accommodation and care for a range of children with different needs. A foster home is classified as a children's home if four or more children are accommodated. Increasingly, specialist children's residential provision is being provided by private agencies, which are required to be registered. Inspection of homes takes place at least twice a year, and all children have the right to make comments about their care to an independent person. The regimes in children's homes vary considerably and have come in for increasing scrutiny since the publication of a series of adverse reports, such as the 'Pindown' report.
c/f Community homes/Foster care/Pindown/Residential care/ Residential schools/Secure accommodation

Children's Panel

The Children's Panel is the Scottish equivalent of the lay-magistrates who preside in English courts. The Children's Hearing system was established in the 1970s after the Social Work (Scotland) Act 1969, and has created an alternative to the juvenile court. Panel members are recruited from the public and efforts have been made to ensure that the 1,500 members are increasingly representative of the communities with which they work. Panel members are appointed by the Secretary of State for Scotland. Three panel members attend a Hearing, one of whom acts as chairperson, plus the Reporter, social worker, at least one parent and the child. Children and families are not subject to the same adversarial process as in a court, since the decision of the panel members is meant to meet the needs of the child in the 'best interests' of that child. The Hearing has no power

Children's Panel (cont'd)

to determine innocence or guilt, and if the grounds for referral are denied, the case must be heard in a Sheriff's court.
c/f Children's hearing/Reporter

Children's Rights

Social welfare is centrally concerned with providing care and protection for children. The 'rights of the child' as they were called by Eglantyne Jebb, the founder of the Save the Children in 1923, focussed on the physical, mental and spiritual rights of children which were later adopted as central parts of the United Nations charter and the Convention on the Rights of the Child 1989.

Children's rights are also enshrined in a wide range of legislation which sets the age(s) at which they are permitted to choose positively to take actions such as own property or possessions; engage in sexual intercourse (age of consent for girls is sixteen); be held responsible for a criminal act (age ten in UK – but much older, fifteen in Germany, and thirteen in France).

Many commentators feel that the rights of children can be categorised as: rights to make decisions, rights to justice, rights to care and protection.

All rights reflect the relationship to power, and legislation has gradually shifted the power for self-control and decision-making away from parents, towards children.
c/f Child protection

Citizen's Charter, The

is a key government statement, which is being used as a model for consumer services, including social welfare. Quality, choice, standards and values are the four central concerns of the Citizen's Charter which will mean for the social services, probation and police, independent quality inspection (auditing) and potentially 'certification' through awarding of 'charter marks' for centres of excellence. The 'perceived service' as experienced by consumers is fundamental to the Citizen's Charter.

The Citizen's Charter as being steadily developed by the Conservative government is principally a means of extending

Citizen's Charter, The

competition and accountability in the public services. The publication of league tables for performance by local authorities in education and health are part of the strategy – but have met with widespread criticism for the way in which figures have been collected. Critics of the government interpretation of the Charter have stressed that the rights of the poor and powerless are not being improved, or are actually being reduced as the Welfare State is being dismantled.
c/f Citizenship/Patient's Charter/Performance standards/Quality assurance/Value analysis

Citizenship

Social welfare workers have been much involved in the debate and issues surrounding the renewed interest in citizenship. The term was first defined fully in 1950 by T H Marshall as 'the rights necessary for individual freedom – liberty of the person, freedom of speech, thought and faith, the right to own property and to conclude valid contracts, and the right to justice'. More recent commentators have stressed that citizenship implies active participation in the community and the State. As a term citizenship means different things to different political writers. Contrary definitions include 'the independence from State Welfare' and 'the social right to welfare for all'.

What is of greatest interest to welfare staff is how citizenship can improve social rights and economic rights in practice, instead of becoming a relatively empty rhetoric. For example, if the Citizen's Charter were to be fully applied to social work it would have implications for user choice and the rights and responsibilities of both consumer and service provider.
c/f Patient's Charter/Welfare state

Claimants

People become claimants when they submit a claim for welfare benefits. The word is particularly used for unemployment benefit claimants who in many parts of the UK have formed themselves into self-help Claimants' Union groups. Social welfare staff often get involved in welfare rights work, and work with the unemployed in unemployed workers' centres and similar schemes.
c/f Benefits/Employment service/Welfare rights

Cleveland

The word 'Cleveland' has crept into common social work use
to mean 'what can go wrong in child protection work' if the
investigation of suspected child abuse becomes over zealous. The
Cleveland report, 1988, under the chair of Elizabeth Butler-Sloss
stressed more care in investigation of abuse and the need for more
data on the extent and nature of child sexual abuse.
c/f Child protection

Client

In social welfare it has been usual to refer to the person or group of
people using or receiving service provision as clients. Client implies
passive receiver, and so in the last few years social welfare agencies
have started to borrow and use the terms *consumer* and *user* to
describe the recipients of services with more control over their own
affairs.
c/f Client trail/Consumer/User

Client-Centred

The move towards seeing the client as an individual with choice and
as a consumer has been enshrined in much government legislation
including the 1989 'Caring for people' (DHSS). The effect of using
social services to empower consumers is to apply quality assurance
techniques in a practical way to make social welfare user-led rather
than service-led.
c/f Child-centred/Client/Quality assurance

Client System

This is a term originating in the systems or unitary model of social
work practice. The client system refers to individuals, groups, or
communities on whose behalf interventions are made, that is the
presumed beneficiaries of the helping effort. The model includes
other kinds of systems, for example, change-agent, target and
action systems, which in conjunction create a particular intervention
strategy.
c/f Clients/Consumers/Systems theory/Target system/Unitary model

Client Trail/Consumer Trail

Client trails are a direct application of the twin concepts of patient trails (from health analysis) and consumer trails (from industry and commerce). A consumer or client trail is a monitoring exercise designed to record exactly what happens to a consumer from their very first point of contact with a social welfare agency. The individual 'trail' may be very complicated and involve a number of agencies. A trail follows the 'career' of a consumer and things an agency will be looking for include: who deals with the consumer? Is the service appropriate and efficient? What records are kept? Was the consumer involved in the design-making process? What were the aims of intervention? What was the consumer view of the service? And, finally, what lessons have been learned, and are there different ways in which a consumer might have been treated?
c/f Performance criteria/Performance indicators

Closed Groups

are specialised, structured groups operating in social work and therapeutic settings. They are viewed as 'closed' by virtue that membership is strictly controlled, with set inclusion criteria, and usually such a group will not admit new members after the group has become established and stable. They are more likely to be organised on a fixed, time limited basis, whereas 'open' groups are more flexible. They are usually facilitated by staff members and can become very mutually supportive for participants. A danger in this type of groupwork is that members can develop too much dependency on the group.
c/f Boundary maintenance/Contracts/Groupwork/Open Groups/ Safeguards

Co-counselling

c/f Peer counselling

Cognitive Ability

is the development of mental ability which allows the natural progression of perception, understanding and evaluation of social phenomena. Child development is based on stages of cognitive

Cognitive Ability (cont'd)

development, first described by Jean Piaget. This includes the dual concepts of *assimilation* and *accommodation* which are central to the development of cognitive ability. These refer primarily to the processes whereby a child receives information and then makes sense of the world, or makes use of the information, accommodating it to prior learning and knowledge. Having a developed cognitive ability is thought to be a useful social welfare skill, especially in counselling work.

Cognitive therapy is also available, which is based on attempts to restructure ways of thinking about personal and interpersonal problems and stress, resulting in new coping skills.
c/f Counselling/Listening skills

Cohort

A cohort is the term in research studies for a group of subjects who were born during a particular time period, or who share common characteristics. It is used in most quantitive research.
c/f Quantitive evaluation/Research

Combination Order

This is a sentence for over-sixteens in criminal proceedings which combines community service with being under the supervision of a probation officer under a Probation Order. It was first established under the 1991 Criminal Justice Act.
c/f Community Service Order/Probation Order/Sentencing

Community Action

is the most politicised and therefore controversial form of community work. Work with tenants and unemployed groups and activists (in such areas as anti-racism and anti-sexism) are examples of community action. As the title suggests, community *action* is about alternative action or strategies to create change. It is often involved with conflict and confrontation and frequently creates tension between staff and their employers over accountability and power. Community work staff who principally see their task as encouraging community action will inevitably be more

Community Action

identified with their communities than their employing authority or organisation.

c/f Community development/Community work

Community-based Services for Elderly People

These cover a range of provision often referred to as 'Home support', 'Day care' and 'Staying put' services. Home support includes help in the home from home helps, provision of meals, and recreation and transport assistance. Day Care services include luncheon and social clubs, recreation and information services and transport to and from the position. Staying put services usually mean adaptation of homes to make them more suitable for an elderly person. Night visiting and alarm call systems can also assist older people to remain in their own homes rather than moving into residential care.

c/f Domiciliary care/Nursing homes/Residential care/Residential care homes

Community Care

has no single official definition. It is used most frequently to describe provision of health and welfare services in a range of diverse, non-institutional settings, including, confusingly, forms of residential and group care.

Informal supports and family networks are two major elements of community care implementation, which stress 'Care in the Community' and 'Care by the Community', rather than the more traditional 'Care for the Community'. The current understanding and use of the phrase was given emphasis by Sir Roy Griffith's report for the government: *Community Care: an Agenda for Action* (HMSO 1988) and the DHSS *Caring for People: Community Care in the Next Decade and Beyond* (HMSO 1969), and in the NHS and Community Care Act (HMSO 1990).

Most significantly, community care implementation should create many more user or consumer-led services; however, the origins of community care go back many decades.

c/f Community work

Community Development

is regarded as a central role of community work, aimed at stimulating local people to help themselves through the acquisition of skills, establishment of new organisations and facilities, and active participation. Community development work in the Third World goes back to the 1920s and had a similar meaning, namely to encourage consciousness-raising and collective participation. Styles of work such as empowerment, enabling and social action can all be seen as part of a community development strategy.
c/f Community action/Community organisation/Community work/ Empowerment

Community Education

is sometimes used to describe all of the local authority youth service and community work services. This is particularly true in Scotland, where the regional education departments provide a community education service. Community Education offers a range of complementary education and recreation opportunities for younger people, sometimes being viewed as social education provision. For adults, community education opportunities include both qualification and vocational or recreational courses and 'second-chance' courses in basic skills. Recreational and leisure opportunities are also provided by some local authorities and voluntary agencies in community centres and other community buildings such as schools and church halls.
c/f Community work/Youth work

Community Homes

The term 'community home' was used following the 1969 Children and Young Persons' Act to describe all forms of residential child care provided by local authorities and voluntary organisations, including the former Approved Schools which became known as Community Homes with Education (CHEs). Recently, community homes of all kinds have been subject to increasing public and professional scrutiny following disclosures of abuse and serious neglect in certain homes. They are regulated by the Children Act 1989 and the Children's Homes Regulations 1991.

Community Homes

Staff recruitment and supervision are under review at the time of writing, following Sir William Utting's report on residential care, published in 1991 and the Warner Report, 1992. Children in community homes are usually subject to either a care order or criminal supervision order. The term *voluntary care* has been replaced by being *looked after in care*.

c/f Looked after/Residential care

Community Mental Health Teams (CMTHs)

These teams offer specialist community resources offering both health promotion and *illness prevention* roles. They are concerned with supporting people in the community, helping to keep them from unnecessarily living or staying in institutions and assisting people on return from hospitals.

Specialist CMTHs include psychogeriatric teams, and teams working with addiction problems, children and families.

c/f Community teams for people with learning difficulties

Community Organisation

is usually used to describe community work *intervention* which helps communities to deal with social problems. Within community organisation, welfare rights facilities and self-help organisations, such as tenants' organisations are representative. Promotion of active participation in education, provision of local facilities and in local government are also central to community organisation as a style of community work.

The term is somewhat vague, and there is, inevitably, overlap in professional and popular use with community development and community action, but it mostly indicates greater organisation and co-ordination of community resources.

c/f Community action/Community development/Community work

Community Ownership

c/f Housing co-operatives

Community Service Orders (CSOs)

are available as a sentence in courts in criminal cases for offenders aged sixteen and over. The purposes of CSOs are as a punishment, as reparation to the community, and to provide some additional benefit to the community. CSOs are supervised by probation staff, but placements can be made in a wide variety of settings and organisations for between 40 and 240 hours in a twelve month period.
c/f Probation/Sentencing

Community Social Work

This refers to the development of localised social services stemming from the Barclay Report (1982). It is linked to the ideas of *patch work* and *neighbourhood work*. The aim is to make social workers much more accessible, visible and ultimately accountable to local communities.

   Whilst it pre-dates the current implementation of community care, it embodies empowerment and is intended to make the most effective use of community networks and resources, in order to address individual and social problems.
c/f Community Care/Patch work/Unitary authority

Community Teams for People with Learning Difficulties (CTLDs)

These teams of professionals are often highly integrated to provide the implementation of 'normalisation' policies and are sometimes known as Community Mental Handicap Teams. Employment and housing assistance as well as advice and counselling can all be part of the team's remit in addition to health-related assistance.
c/f Community mental health teams/Normalisation

Community Work

has no single definition or meaning. It is frequently used to describe all work which takes place outside the formal social services departments. As such, it is a rather vague umbrella term including everything from organising 'good neighbours' self-help schemes, through tenant participation initiatives, to work with young offenders

Community Work

aimed at reducing vandalism. Community work is about supporting individuals and groups in local areas to help themselves. It also relates to making services provided by local authorities and voluntary agencies more relevant, responsive and accountable to local communities.

The organisation of social welfare teams to match 'natural' community boundaries is the usual structure for community work. The number of interventions which may be defined as community work are vast, but the most common distinctive approaches are: community organisation; community development; community action and community education.

c/f Community development/Community workers/Neighbourhood work/Networking

Community Workers

Their tasks are many and various, depending upon the functions and aims of their employing agencies. These tasks normally involve assisting members of a particular community to identify their needs; organise themselves in groups; learn new skills and generally become more self-sufficient and effective. Because they are employed by social services, education and voluntary organisations, the methods used and primary aims also vary considerably. Community workers are particularly involved in encouraging self-help initiatives in areas such as housing, employment, youth work, recreation and community arts. There is a national Association of Community Workers (ACW) which is a membership and campaigning organisation.

c/f Community work/Youth work

Compensation

Offenders under the justice systems operating in the UK can be ordered by the courts in criminal proceedings to pay compensation to the victim of their offence of sums up to £2,000 per offence. Compensation to victims and to society is also made through Community Service Orders, reparation and mediation schemes, and the Criminal Injuries Compensation Board.

Compensation (cont'd)

c/f Atonement/Community Service Order/Compensation Order/ Mediation/Reparation/Victim support

Compensation Order

A compensation order can be made in court up to a ceiling of £2,000 per offence. Under such an order, the offender pays the victim the sum set by the court in criminal proceedings. The offender may also receive other sentences such as fines or a conditional discharge.
c/f Compensation/Reparation

Competence

is the ability to perform work activities to set standards. The notion of competence is closely allied to that of the satisfactory meeting of performance criteria. It refers to the *outcomes* of what people do within a defined role and set of tasks. Competences can accordingly be measured as aspects of performance assessment and appraisal.

Assessment of competences in the work setting by (competent/ qualified/trained) assessors as part of the verification process is one of the basic principles of National Vocational Qualifications.
c/f National Vocational Qualifications

Compulsory Competitive Tendering

as it applies to local government services, is the process of specifying the nature of particular services, which are then advertised for contractual tendering. Contracts are let for fixed lengths of time, usually between three and five years, and services are monitored by the purchasing agency.

Under the successive Conservative governments of Margaret Thatcher and John Major, the introduction of compulsory competitive tendering for many public services has had a radical effect on the management of the personal social services. Social services, housing, education and health departments are now required to request tenders for services ranging from meals, maintenance and repairs to hospital operations and staffing. This makes financial accountability much more important in the daily work of managers, who have to draw up tender documents and decide on suppliers

Compulsory Competitive Tendering

based on price, quality and a range of performance standards. In the era of compulsory competitive tendering, both public and voluntary sector social welfare services are now providers *and* purchasers of services, which should ensure greater choice and quality of service. The implementation of the NHS and Community Care Act specifically requires local authorities as purchasers and commissioners of services, to use 85 per cent of their funds for purchasing services from the private and voluntary sectors. The 1992 Local Government Act has continued to extend CCT to most of the public sector services.

Conceptualisation

is the process by which concepts and ideas are formed as part of a wider process of learning, development and intervention. It describes specific links which a worker (usually at co-ordinating level) sees between, for instance, a client's needs and a means of meeting them. It also describes the decision-making process used to conceptualise, or determine, likely outcomes and the 'best' course of action. Lateral thinking may be involved, for instance in the development of an off-road motor-cycle scheme as an appropriate response for young people involved in traffic offences such as joy-riding.
c/f Groupwork

Conciliation

The main form of conciliation work undertaken by social welfare staff involves disputes between married or unmarried partners. Probation staff, social workers and guardians ad litem are all involved in this work, and much of it relates to the implementation of the 1989 Children Act, which established the legal *responsibilities* of parents and the *rights* of children, and deals with separation orders.

Conciliation work uses counselling methods and listening skills as well as advocacy, often on behalf of the child or children. A number of voluntary organisations are involved in conciliation work, and in particular, RELATE, which is the national marriage guidance council.

Conciliation (cont'd)

Conciliation in employment disputes is sometimes the role of community work staff, and welfare workers who service voluntary management committees.
c/f After-care/Counselling/Guardian ad litem/Probation

Conditioning

is a process used in behaviour modification programmes, particularly those used in work with offenders. *Respondent* or classical conditioning occurs when a stimulus is presented by the worker which conditions or creates a response. *Operant* or *instrumental* conditioning rewards or punishes behaviour. The rewards system of encouraging positive behaviour is well established in the educational contexts of social welfare, with privileges being granted in terms of treats and grades. In offender work, some conditioning programmes are designed to offer alternative models of behaviour which replace delinquent behaviour.
c/f Behaviour modification/Psychology

Conduct Disorders

This is a psychological and psychiatric term used to describe various forms of problematic behaviour particularly in young people. Conduct disorders tend to be grouped around: overactivity or hyperactivity; aggressive destructive behaviour; anti-authority/institutional activities; withdrawn and isolated behaviour. Individual counselling therapy and groupwork may be used to treat the identified disorders by social work staff, psychologists, psychiatrists and so on.
c/f Behaviour modification/Emotional disorders/Groupwork

Conductor

In group therapy circles, the group leader or facilitator is sometimes called the conductor. Usually a conductor will be non-judgemental, non-directive and generally accepting of group members.
c/f Facilitators/Groupwork/Non-directive

Confidentiality

is one of the most frequently discussed concepts in social work. It means agreeing with clients or users not to disclose information about them to third parties. Social workers are not protected by law, and confidentiality is principally an ethic, by which social welfare and health staff try to counsel and advise clients most effectively.
c/f Data protection/Personal information

Consciousness-Raising

This term comes from the work of Paulo Freire in Brazil and Chile. Freire criticised traditional educational and social institutions as being oppressive and narrow in vision. He argued for 'concientization', a process which enables individuals to contribute to the transformation of their worlds. The practical application of this in education and community work has been translated as consciousness-raising, a liberating process encouraging receivers of services to become active partners in the provision and use of such services.
c/f Enabler/Self-actualisation

Consumer

Consumer has been the usual term for purchasers and users of goods in everyday life. This has led to the application of 'consumer' models into social welfare settings, and the term, together with 'user', is now often used instead of *client* to describe those who require services, support and assistance. 'Consumer' used in this way implies that the user has certain rights of choice, and may also be seen in community care as being a partner with the provider in the totality of the service.

It also implies that the 'consumer' has purchasing power, which can be used to satisfy their needs and wants. How far this model of consumerism can be applied to social welfare services is questionable, particularly where the service is compulsorily provided and the consumer has no real power, for instance, offenders.
c/f Client/Client trail/User

Contact Order

Under Section 8 of the Children Act 1989, a new kind of access order called a contact order was established. This is 'an order requiring the person with whom a child lives, or is to live, to allow the child to visit or stay with the person named in that order, or for that person and the child otherwise to have contact with each other'. Contact orders are usually made in cases of divorce or parental estrangement.
c/f Divorce/Residence order

Contagion

Contagion is used by some social work practitioners to describe the power a group can exert over individuals. This power of the group to determine, or strongly influence individual behaviour is sometimes a negative force as in football violence, where emotional contagion is said to affect individual behaviour. Contagion is also present in the activities of sub-groups such as a 'gang', which may be ruled by a charismatic leader whose own violence system is 'contagion'.
c/f Groupwork

Contraception

Social welfare staff may become involved in offering advice in counselling and case work situations either with young people or with parents and their children. The advent of AIDs has encouraged more publicity about 'safe sex' and the use of condoms, and some youth workers encourage discussion on sex and relationships. Social welfare staff may refer children to GPs and clinics for contraception advice. The Gillick judgement has confirmed that children under sixteen can usually seek medical advice on contraception without parental consent. In schools, sex education including information about contraception is controlled by school governors, and in some schools little formal teaching actually takes place.
c/f Family planning/Gillick/Safe sex

Contracting Out

refers to the process whereby many services are put out to compulsory competitive tendering. In social welfare, health and

Contracting Out

housing services, contracting out by local authorities is becoming
commonplace. Local authorities then become purchasers as well
as providers of services and facilities, using both in-house and
outside contractors from the public, private and voluntary sectors.
Residential care services, catering, estate management, maintenance
and laundry services were among the first to be included under the
contracting out arrangements.
c/f Compulsory competitive tendering/Purchaser-provider

Contracts

are oral or written agreements made between one partner and
another. In social work, contracts may be made between worker and
user; between worker and supervisor and between workers and so
forth. In groupwork, contracts may be between all group members
and provide the basis for aims, personal goals, rules and mutual
group boundaries concerning attendance and behaviour.

'Contract' is also used to describe service and financial
agreements between social welfare workers and organisations,
both internally and externally. Contracts of this type are increasingly
important as social welfare organisations become *sellers/providers*
and *purchasers* of services and facilities.
c/f Boundary maintenance/Compulsory competitive tendering/
Groupwork

Control

c/f Social control

Council Housing

c/f Social housing

Counselling

is used to describe a broad range of listening and helping processes
employed in social welfare and health work. The aim is always to
help the person receiving counselling to understand themselves and
their situation better. To be effective, the counsellor must be genuine,
tolerant and empathetic. Counselling is a non-judgemental

Counselling (cont'd)

process and at its heart is listening and allowing the person to offer information at their own pace. Counselling can take place in either structured or unstructured situations, although much social welfare counselling benefits from offering a warm, secure environment in which the process can take place.

Counselling is of particular use when individuals are under pressure, and it encourages the expression of emotions such as grief or anger as a healing experience. Out of the counselling relationship, the person being counselled may also seek information, advice and suggested options. Counselling is frequently used in situations of bereavement, child abuse, drugs and marital breakdown.

c/f Peer counselling/Relate/Therapy

Court Welfare Officers

This is the title given to social work and probation staff who advise the court on welfare considerations in family, care order and other proceedings. Much of their work involves conciliation and producing welfare reports, which have to take particular account of the 1989 Children Act and the Child Support Act.

c/f Welfare reports

Courts

in England and Wales are divided into Criminal and Civil courts, although in fact there is an overlap of functions in certain courts. The main types of courts at which social welfare staff will be expected to attend are: Crown Court (criminal cases); Magistrates Court (criminal or civil cases); High Court (mostly civil cases, and appeals on points of criminal law); County Court (civil cases); Tribunal (civil cases); Court of Appeal (criminal and civil) and House of Lords (final level of appeal on civil and criminal cases).

Most court work involves welfare staff in preparing some form of social inquiry report in cases involving families or children. There are now three types of specialist magistrates' courts: Youth Courts (for up to seventeen year olds in criminal cases); Adult Courts (for adults of eighteen years and over in criminal proceedings); Family Courts (includes care proceedings, adoption, child protection, residence and contact orders).

Courts

In Scotland, the organisation and procedures of courts are significantly different from those in England and Wales. The main courts for criminal and civil proceedings are called Sheriff's Courts. The Sheriff alone judges the facts and the law in most common cases, while in more serious cases a jury judges the facts. The High Court is used for the most serious cases. The Procurator Fiscal decides in which court a case will be tried. Most cases involving young people under sixteen are dealt with by a Children's Hearing.
c/f Children's hearings/Pre-sentence Report/Social inquiry

Co-working

is a method of social work which assists the operation of groups and groupwork by using more than one leader or facilitator. The strength of co-working a group is that participants have more than one role model with which to identify, and facilitators can test out their ideas, share ideas and responsibilities and offer a wider range of expertise and experience. The method is of particular benefit where a mix of gender, age, race or religion are required to enable a group to function effectively. Co-working is sometimes also adapted to individual casework, especially if a worker or consumer requires extra support.
c/f Case and care management/Groupwork

Creche

This is usually a specially run facility for groups of younger children, operated to allow parents to work, take part in an organised event or sports activity. Some employers and retailers offer creche facilities as an incentive to employees and users. Because of the variety of locations in which they are located, creche facilities are harder to regulate than nurseries and child minders.
c/f Child minders/Nursery

Credit Accumulation Transfer (CATs)

CATs are the accumulated credits for units of work successfully completed by candidates on assessable courses, and in particular for those on any of the four basic levels and post-qualifying level on the

Credit Accumulation Transfer (CATs) (cont'd)

National Vocational Qualifications (NVQs) in Social Care. Credits are achieved both through course work approved by training agencies endorsed by the Social Care Consortium, and by work-based assessment of competence.

As a method of student assessment and learning, it has been developed from distance learning courses, where students gain credits from units of work completed, as in the Open University foundation and other courses.

The CATs system as applied to Social Work training is relatively new and is still being developed.

c/f Competence/Distance learning/National Vocational Qualifications

Criminalise

Becoming criminalised occurs when an individual becomes involved in the official system of justice. Intervention from social welfare staff to prevent petty offenders from becoming 'sucked into' the criminal justice system is an important way of counteracting criminalisation. In welfare work, it is common to hear staff refer to a 'criminal career', which refers to the way in which offenders become career criminals, partly because of their backgrounds, and partly through the criminalising and stigmatising effect of being 'in' the system of institutions, courts, contact with the police, contact with other prisoners and so on.

c/f Labelling/Prisoner

Criminal Liability

Under the age of ten a child is not criminally liable for any offence (eight in Scotland). This means that a child cannot be charged or taken to court. Between the ages of ten and fourteen the court must prove that a child has guilty intent – knows what they are doing is wrong. Above fourteen, juveniles are viewed as having full criminal liability for their actions.

Criminology

is defined as the study of the causes, correction and prevention of crime. Criminology is the academic or research-based study

Criminology

of criminal behaviour, but it increasingly involves social welfare staff as they become part of 'systems management' in the justice system. Many social welfare staff work extensively with offenders and ex-offenders in after-care, treatment programmes, employment schemes, education and training schemes, housing projects and safe-neighbourhood schemes; all of which can become the subject of criminological studies.

c/f Gate-keeping/Systems intervention/Systems theory

Crisis Intervention

includes a range of interventions, usually related to a very specific problem or event in an individual's life. The intervention will involve some form of therapeutic casework or groupwork, aimed at helping the client to cope with the 'crisis' and develop strategies for effectively dealing with both the problem and the aftermath.

c/f Brief treatment/Casework/Groupwork/Task-centred casework

Critical Enabling Knowledge

is an arguably over-complicated phrase used in conjunction with the National Vocational Qualifications. It is officially described as 'candidates will need to have enabling knowledge that is *critical* to competent performance in this unit (social care).'

The critical enabling knowledge is, therefore, the knowledge and understanding required by staff in order to perform tasks and enhance skills to do a job to agreed standards.

c/f Competence/National Vocational Qualifications

Critical Incident Analysis (CIA)

A learning and training technique using actual experiences in order to evaluate what has happened. It is used to encourage workers to reflect on their practice and develop powers of self-criticism as part of personal and professional development. To use the technique, workers write down or describe an event of which they were part. It is then analysed in terms of what can be done next. For instance, they then respond to questions such as – 'What did you do?' 'What

Critical Incident Analysis (CIA) (cont'd)

might you have done?' 'What have you learned from the incident?' 'Do you require additional skills or information?' 'What?' 'Prioritise them.'

The exercise can be helpful in staff training and supervision, groupwork, self-help study and so on.

Crown Prosecution Service

This body has taken over from the police the task of evaluating evidence prior to a case being heard in court. In cases where the evidence is weak or where the defendent is very young or old, or infirm, the CP can decide not to pursue a prosecution. The CP is divided into four regions, comprising of 31 areas. Lawyers and barristers handle nearly one and a half million cases per year on behalf of the CP in magistrates and crown courts.

c/f Caution

Curfew Order

This new type of order was introduced by the 1991 Criminal Justice Act for offenders aged sixteen and over. The order can specify a period of between two and twelve hours in any one day for a period of up to six months. It can include electronic tagging or monitoring of offenders during the specified curfew order. Curfew orders can only be made if the offender has accepted the terms of the order. Keeping violent soccer fans away from football grounds is one application of such an order.

c/f Sentencing

Custodial Sentences

describe the range of sentences which place offenders in institutions which restrict their liberty. Young offenders' institutions and prisons are the two main types existing post the 1991 Criminal Justice Act.

c/f Prisons/Young offenders' institutions

Custody

Part II of the Children Act 1989 replaced previous regulations regarding the custody and access to children, following matrimonial

Custody

disputes and divorce. The new legislation created four Section 8
orders which have replaced the old custody order. They are the
residence order; contact order; prohibited steps order, and specific
issue order.

*c/f Conciliation/Contact order/Divorce/Marriage/Prohibited Steps
Order/Residence Order/Specific Issue Order*

D

Data Capture Sheets

Case files are the main source of information collected about any referral to social services agencies. Unfortunately, they can often become overly large! A data capture sheet is a means of condensing all the most important information concerning a case into one document which can be updated. An example of a data capture sheet would include: a) Identifying details; name, case number, and so on, b) Personal details; age, sex, previous case history, c) Reason for referral, d) Decision after assessment, e) Services allocated or received, f) Service changes, g) Case closure, h) Other case events.
c/f Monitoring

Data Protection

Since 1984, any agency or organisation recording personal data must register under the Data Protection Act. There is a charge made for inclusion on the register and legally no person or organisation which is not registered can store personal data. The legislation is probably more often referred to than adhered to, and it seems that many social welfare agencies continue to keep records without fully understanding the law regarding access to records, confidentiality and redress under the 1984 Act.
c/f Confidentiality/Information technology/Recording

Day Care Services for Elderly People

c/f Community-based services for elderly people/Domiciliary care

Deaf and Hearing Impaired People

are entitled to the whole range of service available for physically disabled people. Either directly or through specialist voluntary organisations, social services can provide staff with skills and information to help deaf people cope more effectively in communication, learning, living and employment. A number of national organisations exist to offer support and advice for the deaf,

Deaf and Hearing Impaired People (cont'd)

including the Royal National Institute for the Deaf (RNID); British
Association for the Hard of Hearing, and the British Deaf Association.
c/f Sensory impairments

Decentralisation

Social welfare organisations have tended to become increasingly
decentralised, meaning that they have devolved responsibility
for planning and practice, and in many cases have become
organisationally closer to local communities. It is usually assumed
that decentralisation leads to a more responsive approach to
problems and solutions. It also implies administrative and managerial
changes, for example, devolved budgets, local management of
schools.
c/f Patch work/Unitary authority

Dependency

'Dependency' is used in different contexts. For example, it may
refer to consumers developing a general dependency on the welfare
system, or some particular aspect of it, such as institutional care. It
is usually a major aim of social welfare staff to empower consumers
and to maintain or increase their independence from social welfare
agencies and staff.

Health and drug education work treat the dependency of those
who use or abuse drugs as being either *physical dependency* where
drugs have become an addiction and are used to avoid withdrawal,
or *psychological dependency*, which means that users rely on a drug
to block out or alter reality, to obtain stimulation or pleasure.
c/f Drug use/Institutions/Residential care

Depression

Although more normally dealt with by medical practitioners and
psychiatrists, depression is a condition which many people, including
social welfare consumers, suffer at some time in their lives. If there
is no apparent cause of depression, it is referred to as *endogenous*
depression. *Reactive* depression describes depression which can be
attributed to a cause such as unemployment or bereavement.

Detached Youth Work

is a form of contact work with young people which has been developed by local authorities and voluntary agencies, through education and social work. The workers employed to undertake detached youth work operate principally in neighbourhoods, on streets, and aim to offer relationships and support which enable young people to gain confidence, skills and experience in a non-judgemental way. Workers offer access to resources and information, and can on occasions use counselling and advocacy as methods of work. Contact work is often encouraged with young people on the fringes of crime, at risk and/or abusing drugs.
c/f Directive/Non-directive/Youth work

Detainee

is the term now commonly used for prisoners, and for ex-prisoners receiving services provided through the Employment Department's Training Enterprise and Education Directorate.
c/f Prisoners/Prisons

Diagnostic School

This was a predominantly psychological approach to social work based largely on Freudian theory. As the name implies, proponents stressed the need for careful diagnosis of a client's inner psychological problems in order to develop treatment interventions. The Diagnostic School was influential, particularly in America, from the late 1930s through to the mid-1950s.
c/f Functionalist school

Directive

This term has been used most frequently in relation to the style and method of face-to-face work undertaken in neighbourhood so-called detached work with young people. Directive work implies a worker offering options, challenges and a relatively rigid programme of suggested actions or activities. It also suggests taking a more intrusive and interventionist role with consumers. In the 1990s, being directive may have slight pejorative overtones which makes it untenable alongside empowerment and partnership working,

Directive (cont'd)

although some activity based work with social welfare clients will always be directive by the nature of institutionalised relationships. Responsibility for buildings and accountability to managers and funders create a necessity for directive relationships in a number of social welfare settings, especially in areas like Intensive Intermediate Treatment where changing offending behaviour is a frequent goal.

c/f Detached youth work/Non-directive

Disablement Resettlement Officers (DROs)

These officers work with disabled people who have work related problems. They perform a range of functions including giving advice on rehabilitation, training schemes, employment options, and the registration of disabled people under the provisions of the Disabled Persons (Employment) Act 1944. Their work is particularly important for recently disabled people who face difficulties in adjusting to disability. They are usually based in jobcentres.

c/f Jobcentre

Disability

'A person with disability' is the term preferred by many disabled people to *handicapped*, *invalid* or *person with special needs*, to describe both the impairment suffered by individuals and the disadvantages caused by organisations which take little or no account of the needs of disabled people.

c/f Mental handicap/Normalisation/Special needs

Disclosure

A disclosure interview takes place in child protection work and is a therapeutic device used to get children to talk about difficult and painful experiences. The Memorandum of Good Practice (Home Office, 1992) recommends the use of an interview technique called 'Stepwise' which has four stages: rapport, free narrative, questioning and closure. The concept of disclosure implies that the person interviewed has something to hide and many commentators have

Disclosure

criticised the assumption that social work investigation should seek 'undisclosed' information as an aim.

c/f Child protection

Discretion

Local authorities have discretion to supply/make available certain services and facilities, but this discretion can also be extended to their individual clients. So, in practice even a service the local authority is obliged to make available, can be withheld on the discretion of the local authority if the individual is not seen as needing the service.

The social services, housing departments and police all have considerable power to exercise 'discretion', which may or may not benefit their clients.

Fully discretionary services include meals on wheels for the elderly and schemes for expectant mothers.

c/f Caution/Obligation/Vulnerable people

Discrimination

This is usually used to describe the negative or positive ways in which groups or categories of people are treated differently. The different treatment can be as a result of gender, race, religion, class, disability or economic position, and may be institutionally reinforced in sets of rules, or ways in which statistics are collated, which gives rise to indirect discrimination. Positive discrimination in social work usually means that individuals or groups of consumers receive or can request services not available to others in the wider community. Community Development programmes, Urban Aid and the Social Fund are examples of positive discrimination which is intended to *compensate*, but can on occasions further *label* people and disempower them.

Anti-discriminatory policy and practice often embodied in equal opportunities policies help combat any behaviour or activity which discriminates by race, disability, age, sexuality or religion.

c/f Equal opportunities/Labelling/Racism

Disposal

Making a disposal is the rather de-humanising term used for the action applied to an individual in any particular social work case. For instance, welfare staff may refer to making a disposal 'into care'! The term is used especially by researchers and planners who monitor social welfare systems, measuring the treatment and services used and the outcomes or effectiveness of the intervention. This is often expressed in terms of certain numbers of disposals or alternative disposals, which describe possible service options. 'Disposal' is often used synonymously with the word *referral*.
c/f Process recording/Referral

Distance Learning

is used in situations where trainees and students have to study or work largely on their own. Materials for distance learning are specially developed to enable self-programmed learning and may form part of a course or study programme. Where distance learning is flexible and experiential it is often called Open Learning.
c/f Open learning

Diversion

has become used, especially in work with juvenile justice, as a term to describe interventions which prevent inappropriate, formal or intrusive action being taken. Diversions, for instance, through police warnings can prevent offenders being processed and offer them 'one last chance' to avoid formal proceedings. This type of diversion can occur as a policy procedure in social services departments to check actions taken by staff which would move clients into formal provision which is too controlling or punitive.
c/f Gate-keeping/Systems intervention

Divorce

is the legal termination of a marriage once it has irretrievably broken down. One of the partners must prove this to be the case based on one of the five grounds laid down under the 1973 Matrimonial Causes Act. These include unreasonable behaviour, adultery, desertion and separation. The newly established Child Support

Divorce

Agency, set up under the Child Support Act 1991, will deal with the assessment of and enforcement of maintenance orders.

Under the 1989 Children Act are to be found most of the legal principles determining cases where there is dispute over the future of a child following relationship breakdown. Probation and social services staff become involved in assessing cases coming before court, taking the child's best interests as paramount.
c/f Conciliation/Marriage

Domiciliary Care

is an increasingly outmoded term describing a range of services in the community, as opposed to residential care. It was frequently used to describe support provided for elderly and disabled people living in their own homes but needing assistance through home-helps, meals-on-wheels and Good Neighbours schemes. In the 1990s, the impetus of the NHS and Community Care changes have led to *community care* being used, arguably inappropriately, as the replacement term for domiciliary care. However, community care is really a much wider term that can incorporate some aspects of residential care in addition to 'home care'.
c/f Community-based care for the elderly/Community care/Good neighbours/Home helps/Meals-on-wheels

Drug Dependence

This term applies to the millions of people who have developed a dependency upon a wide range of drugs, including stimulants such as caffeine which is in tea and coffee, nicotine in tobacco, alcohol and prescribed medicines such as sleeping drugs. The controlled drugs, including illegal drugs such as LSD, heroin and cannabis, are generally regarded as having high potential for physical and psychological dependence.
c/f Dependency/Drug use/Health education

Drug Education

Preventative drug education has long been a controversial subject. Schools, parents and social welfare staff have frequently been

Drug Education (cont'd)

reluctant to develop any sort of systematic programme, and have often relied upon 'one-off' lectures and the occasional information leaflet. This approach has now largely been replaced by a more positive strategy which sees drug education as an intrinsic part of health education within the National Curriculum. Drug education is often described as being aimed at: 1) providing accurate knowledge, 2) exploring attitudes and feelings, 3) encouraging the development of self-confidence and social skills.

c/f Dependency/Drug dependence/Drug use/Health education

Drug Use

Work relating to drug use and abuse is one aspect of social welfare work. A drug is any substance which alters the way in which the body functions. Social welfare interventions have included prevention campaigns based on 'Just say no', through shock-horror strategies, to interventions for minimising damage by offering needle exchanges and non-judgemental advice, information and therapy. Drug education work is usually most effective when it is organised by multi-agency teams offering inputs from education, social work and health staff. It also works best when the approach uses empowerment of people as a means of helping them to make informed decisions about their use of drugs and their attitudes towards the use or misuse of drugs and health as a whole. Drugs are frequently categorised in relation to their legality and social acceptability; caffeine, alcohol and tobacco being examples of legally available and quite acceptable drugs which still produce levels of physical and psychological dependency.

c/f AIDs/Dependency/Empowerment/Health education

Dyslexia

is a disorder which impairs reading and writing skills. People with dyslexia do not usually suffer from any other restrictions in learning ability. However, they can find learning difficult because of their failure to recognise certain letters and words, and to organise sequences of words. In some cases there is a tendency to reverse the order of letters.

E

Educational Grants Advisory Service (EGAS)

Run by the Family Welfare Association, an independent voluntary organisation, this is a specialist advice service for intending students and students already in higher or further education. Loans, grants and awards all exist as potential sources of funding for students.

Education Supervision Order (ESO)

Section 36 of the Children Act 1989 established a specific order to look after the welfare of children in cases involving school non-attendance. Education departments apply for an Education Supervision Order (ESO) but *must* consult with the social services department.

An ESO lasts initially for one year but can be extended for up to three years and involves a supervisor, who is usually an Education Welfare Officer, advising and befriending both child and parent in order to secure proper education. If the child or parent ignores the supervisor under an ESO, criminal proceedings may be taken or the social services may investigate the case.

c/f Education Welfare Officer/Sentencing/Supervision Order

Education Welfare Officer (EWO)

The 1988 Education Reform Act signalled the need for increasing co-operation between Education Welfare Officers and social workers in cases relating to school welfare and attendance. The nature and role of EWOs continues to be subject to debate and the relationship between EWOs, social workers, educational psychologists and child guidance staff varies between local authorities. The operation of the new Education Supervision Order will test the EWO system as truancy continues to present a major problem in many areas of the UK.

c/f Education Supervision Order

Elder Abuse

The mistreatment, neglect or exploitation of older people either by individuals, by organisations or institutions is known as elder abuse. Increasing concern has been voiced about the treatment of older people in residential care and in domestic situations where elderly relatives have come to be regarded as a nuisance. The extent of the problem is unknown and relatively little research has been undertaken in this area.

c/f Older people

Elderly People

c/f Older People

Emergency Protection Order

An Emergency Protection Order (EPO) is an emergency response aimed at protecting children where there is 'reasonable cause to believe that the child is likely to suffer significant harm' (Children Act 1989, section 44). Any person, not necessarily a local authority or the NSPCC can apply to a magistrate or court for an EPO, but in practice the application is usually made by a local authority or the NSPCC. An EPO lasts for up to eight days and may involve the child being looked after in local authority accommodation while the circumstances are investigated.

Parents or the child can apply after 72 hours to have the EPO discharged, allowing for 'right of challenge' to the order and the case on which it is based.

c/f Care/Care order/Child Assessment Order

Emotional Disorders

The term refers to a range of emotional problems, which psychiatrists classify as emotional disorders. These include depression, anxiety, phobias (fears) and obsessive behaviour. Helping young people, in particular, come to terms with, and overcome these emotional difficulties is often a major part of counselling, therapeutic and groupwork interventions.

c/f Conduct disorders/Depression

Empathy

Having empathy is often referred to as a basic social work or social care skill. It describes that ability to understand another person's situation and possibly their feelings, *and* be able to communicate that sense of understanding (empathy). It does not necessarily mean that a staff member will agree with the person or client with whom they are working. Empathy is a particularly crucial skill in counselling work, and especially in crisis situations such as child abuse, bereavement, and relationship break-ups.
c/f Counselling/Listening skills

Employment Rehabilitation Centres (ERCs)

Twenty five ERCs are provided nationally by the government as part of the rehabilitation service for people who are disabled or who have been ill. Each centre includes a commercial workshop, and staff are multi-professional, including an occupational psychologist, a nurse, a social worker, a resettlement officer and a chief rehabilitation instructional officer. They are designed to help prepare people for open employment, where possible.
c/f Employment rehabilitation service/Vocational rehabilitation

Employment Rehabilitation Service

This is the national rehabilitation service for people who have been ill or are disabled. As part of the Employment Service, it provides (in 1993), twenty five Employment Rehabilitation Centres; six ASSET Centres (Assistance Towards Employment); two ACTs (Assessment and Counselling teams); and thirty Mobile Assessment teams. Social workers are employed as part of the service personnel as are psychologists and nurses.

Special training and assessment are among the services provided.
*c/f ACTs/Asset centres/Employment rehabilitation centres/
Employment service/Mobile assessment teams*

Employment Service (ES)

The Employment Service provides Jobcentres and Benefit Offices. These provide a network of services for those seeking work,

Employment Service (ES) (cont'd)

including advice on career options and payment of benefits to
unemployed people who are entitled to claim.
c/f Training, Enterprise and Education Directorate

Employment Training (ET)

Employment training initiatives offer vocational training intended
to help unemployed people get back into work. Many courses
lead to national vocational qualifications in a variety of trades and
professions. Long term unemployed people are prioritised for ET
opportunities, particularly eighteen to twenty four year olds who have
been out of work for six to twelve months and eighteen to forty nine
year olds who have been registered unemployed for over two years.
Priority is also given to certain special needs groups such as certain
ex-offenders, people with disabilities and people requiring literacy or
numeracy support.
c/f Employment service/Training and Enterprise Councils (TECs)

Employment With Remploy (REMPLOY)

Since the 1944 Disabled Persons (Employment) Act, employment
with Remploy has provided sheltered employment for severely
handicapped people. At present, nearly 9,000 people are employed
in over 90 production units. The Employment Service provides
grant aid towards capital and employment costs. Disablement
Resettlement Officers at local jobcentres help to assess and recruit
suitable people to work for Remploy.
c/f Vocational rehabilitation

Empowerment

is the current 1990s phrase, to describe enabling clients and
consumers of social welfare services to have more power and
control over matters and issues affecting their lives. It is closely
linked in community care to *partnership working*, which encourages
professionals to work as partners with their clients. It is usually cited
as both an *aim* for social welfare staff and a *means* for them to
achieve that aim. Linked words which involve the transfer of power to
disadvantaged individuals and groups include *enfranchisement,*

Empowerment

enabling, citizenship, facilitation and *animation*. Advocacy may be used as one specific means of empowering people directly or indirectly.
c/f Advocacy/Animation/Citizenship/Enablers/Enfranchisement/ Facilitation

Enabler/Enabling

is a frequently used term to describe ways in which social care staff encourage clients to build on their personal strengths and to overcome difficulties, problems and personal weaknesses. Enabling techniques include *problem-solving, active-listening* and *facilitation*. *Action-centred learning* and *experiential learning* are further examples of what is often called the enabling role. In layman's terms, enabling is the process of helping people to optimise their potential and find the most effective means of helping themselves.
c/f Facilitator

Enabling Body

This is the term used to describe the organisation, which may be a local authority, which supports and actively assists consumers to purchase and use available resources and services. In the housing field, local authorities who have taken part in the voluntary transfer of housing stock to housing associations and other alternative landlords, are now fulfilling the role of enabling bodies. This marks a change from being landlords, to enabling through strategic planning; housing need; special needs; homelessness; budgeting, and monitoring and inspection. It seems likely that other personal social services will follow this trend and become enabling authorities rather than direct providers.
c/f Enabler/Externalisation/Voluntary transfer

Epistemology

is a word which is occasionally found in social welfare writing, especially in academic research findings. It means 'theory and science of knowledge', and is used to describe a body of knowledge which belongs to a particular profession or academic discipline.
c/f Paradigm

Equal Opportunities

is an important aspect of social welfare work and most agencies are committed to providing equal opportunities in employment to their staff and equal opportunities to services and facilities for consumers. The legal obligations are embodied in the Race Relations Act 1976, The Sex Discrimination Acts of 1975 and 1986 and the Disabled Persons (Employment) Acts of 1944 and 1958. A comprehensive equal opportunities policy includes actively encouraging training on related issues and attitudes; anti-discriminatory practice and policies including actively opposing any form of sexual or racial harassment, ageism, cultural or religious discrimination, and promotion of language use, which is free of gender or racial bias.
c/f Ageism/Discrimination/Racism/Sexism

Escort

is the increasingly used term to describe the person who accompanies prisoners or young people under supervision orders, when they are being transferred between different residential establishments. Young people who abscond are also subject to being escorted back to the source institution. Private escort agencies are now frequently tendering for this work, which has caused some controversy in both professional circles and the media.
c/f Prison/Young offenders' institutions

Estate Action

is one of three government initiatives to try and tackle the problems created by poorly designed and built housing estates. They represent a form of positive discrimination concentrating resources into the worst estates where the greatest need exists. A variety of schemes are being piloted including homesteading which aims to offer those in housing need, property requiring repair and renovation, and in exchange homesteaders receive lower rents or a reduced price for the purchase of the property.
c/f Homesteading/Housing action trusts/Priority estates project/Social housing

Ethnic Minority/Ethnic Group

Any group of people who share customs, race, language, origin or traditions are frequently referred to as an ethnic group. Sometimes, the term is used more distinctly to describe particular racial groups, but complex groups such as Romanies and New Age Travellers also consider themselves persecuted as minority group members.

Welfare work with ethnic groups always runs the risk of paternalism, and professional practice needs careful consideration of cultural perspectives and a non-judgemental approach.
c/f Racism

Evaluation

implies a systematic process of information collection regarding aims; costs; service delivery; user-views; outcomes and comparisons between outcomes and aims. The evaluation of social welfare services will inevitably concentrate on the prioritisation of services: the quality of service provided and the value for money of any service. One model of evaluation being proposed for social welfare service purposes involves: measurement of quantities; description of qualities (what is actually provided); judgement on performance standards (set against policy statements and values). Standards are set by someone and are therefore subjective.
c/f Monitoring/Value analysis

Evidence

The job of a social worker in making a case which may be presented to court is one of acting in the best interests of the individual client, by assessing need in the context of available resources. The evidence collected by the social worker usually comes from interviews and records produced by other professionals. The social enquiry report (SER/SIR) is the most frequently used form of social work 'evidence', but various forms of assessment reports are also utilised.
c/f Admissibility/Social enquiry/Social inquiry reports

Evidence from Past Achievements (EPA)

is the unwieldy phrase used for assessment of a candidate's or student's previous work and experience, particularly in relation to the

Evidence from Past Achievements (EPA) (cont'd)

National Vocational Qualifications. In the NVQs the same process is more usually called the accreditation of prior learning.
c/f Accreditation of prior learning

Experiential Learning

is a technique now much favoured in social welfare training and staff development which actively encourages participants to share and evaluate their 'here and now' personal experience, as a means of learning more effectively. The purpose is to learn from the process and change and modify personal behaviour and attitudes as a result. This type of learning is participative, and facilitators encourage participants to 'own' their training and learning.
c/f Accreditation of prior learning

Explicate

is a term meaning literally to explain or to develop an idea or theory. It is more often used by sociologists and in academic writing than in social welfare, professional writing.

Extended Family

is the name given to the wider network of relations of the nuclear or core family group. This can include grandparents, uncles, aunts, cousins, and so on.
c/f Family

Externalise

has a variety of meanings, but the most common is in the context of counselling and therapy work with young people and bereaved. Counsellors help individuals or small groups to externalise their feelings. With young people, it is the distinction they make between themselves and the environment in which they live.

Externalisation

In the 1990s, the term externalisation has been used for the development of new suppliers or providers who are taking on former local authority responsibility for a wide range of social welfare

Externalisation

services. The use of compulsory competitive tendering (CCT) and the development of voluntary agencies has meant that local authority social work, housing and other services are increasingly regarded as the central regulating agencies. This leaves the service provision function to be provided by voluntary and commercial organisations.

c/f Compulsory competitive tendering/Contracting out/Enabling body

F

Face to Face Work

is a commonly used phrase to describe work undertaken by staff working with clients or consumers. It is also sometimes referred to as *coal-face work* and *fieldwork*, to differentiate it from administrative and managerial tasks.

Facilitators/Facilitation

The facilitator role is virtually synonymous with that of the *enabler*, and the facilitation process is an active form of assistance for consumers. The facilitator will, at different times, act as a source of ideas and information; help empower through negotiation, advocacy and mediation, and generally act as an encouraging, positive influence. Facilitation is sometimes used as the term to describe the activity of *networking*, where service and service users are put in touch with each other, through formal or informal networks.

In essence, it is about activity which aids positive change to occur, and is often used in the context of training, and also in self-help strategies.

c/f Empowerment/Enabler/Groupwork/Networking

Family/Families

The family is regarded as the central unit for social organisation by the majority of people. The family group consists of members related by blood, adoption, marriage or friendship in closed, *nuclear* arrangements and in more diverse, extended kinship patterns. The institutional base of the family through partners taking marriage vows is traditionally meant to act as a long-term bond, either by choice or sometimes by arrangement. However, family violence, infidelity and innumerable personal, social and economic problems have increased the incidence of separation and divorce at least in Western societies.

Social welfare staff frequently deal with the effects of these social problems – isolation, depression, bereavement, mental illness, disturbed behaviour, alcohol and drug abuse. Family work is at the

Family/Families (cont'd)

core of social work practice whether it is in the area of preventative work with children and potentially abusive parents, or interventions designed to prevent injury and harm to family members and help all in need.

The family itself is usually constituted as a group living in a single household. Children are socialised and experience their primary educational learning through the family. When children are taken into care by the local authority, it is their responsibility to provide an equivalent of family care.

c/f Conciliation/Divorce/Family groupwork/Group work/Marriage

Family Assistance Order

This has replaced the old matrimonial supervision order made under the Children and Young Persons Act 1969. Section 1 of the Children Act 1989 established this new type of court order, which is designed to be used only in exceptional circumstances for up to six months. It offers the assistance of a social worker or probation officer to family members, and is a voluntary measure only made with the consent of those involved. The aim is usually to support and befriend the members of the family and particularly children, during transitional periods, especially in divorce and adoption cases, and family court proceedings.

c/f Sentencing/Supervision Order

Family Credit (FC)

is a state benefit available to low income families where one member of the family is working for at least 16 hours per week. It is governed by the Social Security Act 1986 and the Family Credit (General) Regulations 1987. It is only available to parents with a dependent child.

c/f Housing benefit/Income support

Family Groupwork

Work with family groups is usually a form of preventative work to reduce isolation, alienation and intolerance. Family groupwork has become a way of tailoring social work intervention to local

Family Groupwork

community needs. In some cases social workers act as group workers, in others family groups are established by social workers, but are run by local people for local people.

The term is used to describe different types of group – sometimes it is counselling and therapeutic work with a nuclear family – at other times it refers to a group of between eight and twelve people from a local area with their children. Some groups have closed membership and contracts, others are very flexible and may be open to any self-referral, rather than being referred by social services or any other statutory or voluntary agency.

c/f Closed groups/Conciliation/Contracts/Family/Groupwork/Open groups/Self-help

Family Placement

is the term used for foster care arrangements made by a local authority social services department. Children whose parents or guardians cannot look after them may be placed with another family under a private arrangement, or may be subject to a foster placement organised by the local authority. Families and their accommodation are assessed by local authority staff and preference is given to families of similar ethnic background, race and religion.

c/f Adoption/Foster care

Family Planning

This is a responsibility of the district health authorities, who are responsible both for giving advice on contraception, making medical examinations and supplying various forms of contraception. Family planning advice and treatment is also supplied through a whole range of voluntary organisations, including the Family Planning Association, the Brook Advisory centres which are sited in many parts of the UK, and particularly deal with counselling on emotional and sexual problems for people under twenty five years old. Social workers often support and advise clients regarding where they can also receive family planning advice in their local area.

c/f Contraception/Gillick

Family Therapy

covers a range of interventions designed to help families cope with stress and problems. Social workers, psychiatrists and psychologists and voluntary agencies all involve themselves in forms of family therapy. Therapeutic techniques are used with the whole family group and focus on inter-personal relationships, roles, and verbal and non-verbal interaction. Intervention can employ methods based on systems theory, psychosocial therapy and behavioural modification.

Family therapy tends to focus on the relationships and behaviour patterns and attitudes of the family group. This contrasts with interventions which focus on individual problems. This type of therapy has aroused some criticism for being culturally insensitive to certain types of disadvantaged, and non-conforming family groups.

c/f Psychology/Psychosocial/Therapy

Family Violence

The cause and prevention of family violence is an increasing concern of social welfare staff. Child abuse, battering of women, alcohol and drug abuse and mental illness, along with social and economic factors – lack of money, inadequate housing and unemployment – can all be seen as linked.

Social work responses to family violence take two main forms:

a) Interventions designed to reduce or prevent violence. This can be through counselling, group work and activity programmes which offer positive alternatives to potentially violent behaviour. Some preventative programmes are focused on particular geographical areas such as run down housing estates and are aimed at giving community members more involvement and optimism.

b) Responses to violence may also include counselling and therapy. The nature of these social work interventions are necessarily varied according to the needs of the perpetrator and victim, abuser and abused.

c/f Counselling/Family/Family groupwork/Priority estates project/ Relate

Field Worker

is the commonly used name for all welfare staff members who actively work in hands-on, but non-clerical situations, directly with social welfare consumers. Fieldworkers will most usually not have management responsibilities and are increasingly likely to hold some form of professional qualification.
c/f Social worker

Focusing

is used to describe a process in counselling, where the counsellor assists the client to look at specific aspects of their problem or situation. For instance, the client might be asked to identify a) what they feel to be their most significant problem, and b) agree to talk about it, then c) identify a strategy to deal with the problem, and d) identify further areas of difficulty, and repeat the process.

Focusing used in this sense is a form of prioritisation.
c/f Counselling/Summarising

Force Field Analysis

is a technique for analysing the need for change in any organisation (such as improving performance or cutting costs). The forces existing to prevent or limit change are then considered, such as staff fears or lack of competence. The analysis then produces an action plan designed to be used to effect change and achieve organisational goals.

Formative Evaluation

is used in research programmes as a development tool to provide feedback and analysis of what is going on, and what needs to be changed to improve effectiveness. Information collected as part of a monitoring process can contribute to this formative evaluation.
c/f Monitoring/Summative evaluation

Foster Care

is governed by the Children Act 1989 and the Foster Placement (Children) Regulations 1991. The local authority social services department regulates both privately arranged foster care

Foster Care (cont'd)

arrangements and family placement of children directly the responsibility of the local authorities. Fostering occurs when a child's parents or guardian are unable to provide care and support, or have become subject to a court order. Arrangements under a care plan for the accommodation of the child will use foster care families wherever possible. Carers are assessed as to their suitability for children of different ages and sex, and their households are inspected. No household normally fosters more than three children.
c/f Adoption/British Agencies for Adoption and Fostering/Community homes/Family placement

Functionalist School

This was a distinct theoretical and practical theory of social work which is also known as the 'Pennsylvania School'. It developed many adherents in the period 1930–1950, based particularly on the psychological work of Otto Rank, who emphasised the importance of the individual 'will'. The Functional School advocated time limited intervention specifically focused on the presenting problem.
c/f Diagnostic school

G

Gaming

Gaming in social welfare is applied to specialist role plays or simulations where social situations are used as 'games' with special rules and roles. Gaming is used as a means of learning about what has happened, what might happen and how staff may be better prepared or trained for various eventualities.
c/f Role-play/Simulation

Gate-keeping/Gate-keeper

are terms used in at least two different social work contexts. Gate-keeping is used to describe the activities of monitoring and diverting individuals from court, through the use of the police warning system and by 'no-action' responses by the Reporter to the Children's Panel in Scotland; and diversion from custody by use of community based alternatives to custodial sentencing.

Gate-keeping can also involve senior or principal social services staff acting as a *gate* or *check* in the system of social work and probation reports to courts or Children's Hearings. This is aimed at preventing inappropriate allocation of resources. An example of gate-keeping would be where the Director of Social Services personally vets any Social Inquiry Reports (SIRs) which recommend a residential supervision order. Gate-keeping can also indicate a positive role of allocating resources and services based on need.
c/f Community based alternatives/Diversion/Systems intervention

Gateway

Gateway is the name given to the service provided by jobcentres for job-seekers and employers. The 'Gateway' offers information on the entire range of training, employment and enterprise opportunities.
c/f Employment service/Jobcentre

GBH/ABH

These initials are often used instead of the full words for serious assaults: Grievous Bodily Harm and Actual Bodily Harm.

Generic

The term, strictly speaking, refers to the common base or framework of values, knowledge networks and skills which underpin *all* social work practice. However, in practice, it has tended to become confused and synonymous with the ideas of *generalist* social work, meaning the application of 'generic' knowledge and skills to a variety of social problems and situations. In this sense it is the opposite of specialist work, which focuses on particular user groups, and uses specialist methods and sets of skills.

Generic social workers take on a complete mixture of clients' cases, normally working from an area office and serving a particular geographical community (patch), with a wide range of approaches.
c/f Case-management/Casework/Specialist

Genogram

This is a technique for portraying family relationships in a family tree type representation. Genograms are used by probation and social work staff with their clients to provide a map of family and friendship patterns. Using a genogram can uncover difficult-to-obtain information from shy or obstructive clients and may unblock threatening or difficult staff-client relationships. However, it can also unleash powerful emotional responses and must be handled with care and sensitivity.
c/f Recording

Gerontology

Gerontology is the study of ageing, but as applied to welfare work, it is the practical provision of specialist services to assist older people. With the demographic shift towards an ageing population, more social welfare staff are involved with directly providing services for older people, or purchasing the range of social, health and accommodation services.
c/f Older people

Gestalt Therapy

Gestalt literally means 'whole' and the therapy is designed to help individuals deal more effectively and realistically with their problems

Gestalt Therapy

as a holistic process. Within the therapy, individuals are encouraged to become more aware of their actions, feelings and gestures and to take ownership or responsibility for them. Therapy can take place in groups led by a directive group leader, who encourages communication through contact. Gestalt therapy was developed by Laura and Frederick Perls, and it is used particularly in mental health groups.
c/f Directive/Holistic/Self-actualisation/Therapy

Gillick

The Gillick ruling by Lord Scarman in the House of Lords in 1988 has influenced social work practice in counselling and advising children under sixteen on contraception. The ruling stated that 'the parental right to determine whether or not their minor child below the age of 16 will have medical treatment terminates if and when the child achieves a sufficient understanding and intelligence to enable him or her to fully understand what is proposed'.
c/f Contraception/Family planning/Safe sex

Good Neighbours

Schemes run under the heading 'Good Neighbours' are often actively encouraged through social welfare agencies. These may involve the informal or formal networking of people in a particular community, with the aim of encouraging the support for, and setting up of care systems, on a self-help basis. They are particularly successful in protecting and liberating vulnerable, elderly people who may feel trapped or isolated in their homes.
c/f Community Care/Community development/Neighbourhood work/Networking

Grief Work

c/f Bereavement/Counselling

Griffiths

Published under the title: *Community Care; Agenda for Action* (HMSO DHSS) in 1988, Roy Griffiths' report has genuinely

Griffiths (cont'd)

established much of the agenda for change in social services. The main thrust of the report was to recommend that local authority social services should direct and purchase services rather than provide them. There was also a range of recommendations designed to support more community-based and home-based care as an alternative to residential care. The government reaction and implementation of some of the Griffiths' proposals were embodied in *Caring for People* (DHSS 1989) and the *NHS and Community Care Act* (HMSO 1990).
c/f Community care

Groupwork/Social Groupwork

This is a traditional method of social work, alongside casework and community work. Groupwork includes structured 'open' and 'closed' groups where social work staff expect group interaction to benefit the participants. Groupwork usually has a range of agreed *techniques* (exercises, games, shared experiences, discussions, information exchange); *aims* (behaviour change, skill development, confidence building) and will rely on the *skills* of the group leader(s) to enable group interchanges to be handled sensitively and in ways which encourage personal and group growth. It is usually seen as complementary to individual assessment and supervision. There are a number of groupwork theories and models.
c/f Closed groups/Open groups/Safeguards

Guardian Ad Litem (GAL)

The term 'Guardian ad litem' (GAL) is Latin and little understood outside of the legal profession. It is the role and task of a GAL in child protection cases, where there is likely to be a conflict of interests between the adults involved and the child, to protect the best interests of the child. This is of paramount importance.
c/f Care order/Child protection/Supervision order

H

Half Way House

is a commonly used, rather loose term, to describe a range of temporary accommodation for people leaving various forms of institutional residential care. Prisoners, ex-patients with a history of mental illness, alcoholics, drug addicts and homeless people are amongst the categories sometimes accommodated in half way housing. The 'half way' of the phrase relates to the housing being in between institutions or specialist care and normal rented or purchased housing stock.

c/f Hostels/Residential care

Hardware

'Computer-speak' has begun to slip into general and social welfare use. 'Hardware' is used to describe any physical piece of computing equipment – monitor, terminal, computer, printer, keyboard, and so on. It is now becoming fashionable to apply it to any other physical equipment such as photocopiers, fax machines, transport and office furniture.

c/f Software

Health Care

is the term applied both to the network of services and personnel providing a diverse range of health provision and to the individual care and treatment of people suffering from physical and mental disorders. At its widest, 'Health care' describes the entire system of prevention through primary care intervention, and all secondary interventions designed to detect and treat health problems and disorders. This includes all buildings with a health function from clinics and doctors' surgeries through to hospitals and hospices. Social workers are particularly active in child protection, cases involving AIDs and mental health, where frequently they are part of multi-agency or multi-disciplinary teams.

c/f Social care

Health Education

is increasingly accepted as the responsibility of a range of social welfare and education staff rather than the specialist function of health professionals. Health education involves sharing information and offering experiences and stimulation to all members of society which inform their choices regarding physical, social and mental well-being.
c/f Drug use/Health care

Health Promotion

c/f Health education

Helping

Social care and welfare staff provide a variety of interventions which are specifically aimed at 'helping' clients or consumers. Helping may include: empathy and understanding; listening; self-advocacy; counselling and therapy; assessment and treatment programmes. Because of the variable nature of the staff-user relationship, some 'help' may be unasked for and actually viewed negatively, particularly in situations such as residential care where help may be intrusive.
c/f Advocacy/Counselling/Empathy/Listening skills

Her Majesty's Inspectors (HMIs)

These are the Inspectors of Schools who may inspect and advise establishments providing education. This includes social care facilities where schooling is part of the service provided and residential schools which are also regulated under the Children Act 1989 by social service departments. HMIs are also responsible for the inspection of youth and community facilities and colleges. They are employed by the Department of Education and Science.
c/f Residential schools

HIV

stands for Human Immuno-deficiency Virus, the virus which can destroy the immune system and result in the condition known as AIDs. HIV infection symptoms can include: fever, heavy night sweats, unexplained weight loss, chronic fatigue, diarrhoea, oral thrush,

HIV

herpes and bleeding gums. Obviously, these symptoms can exist in many people who have not contracted the HIV virus. The virus is usually contracted through sex, sharing needles, breast milk and infected blood.

HIV testing looks for the presence of antibodies (proteins) in the blood. A positive result indicates the existence of the virus, HIV positive; a negative result shows that the virus is not present, or that the antibodies have not yet developed.
c/f AIDs

Holistic/Holism

This model offers an approach which considers the whole of a person or phenomenon. Problems are not seen in isolation, and the model uses a highly integrated methodology, utilising any available theories and styles of work. Holistic models of work in medicine and social welfare tend to favour approaches 'in balance' with the environment, and the emphasis is on seeing the individual in the context of all social, cultural, physical and psychological influences.
c/f Unitary model

Home Helps

are employed by local authorities to provide a range of domestic help for elderly people, disabled, the sick and maternity cases. Cleaning, cooking and shopping are the traditional services, but in some cases, personal care – help with dressing, bathing and mobility – is also provided.
c/f Community based services for elderly people/Domiciliary care

Home Life

This is the name of a semi-official, and very influential code of practice for the running, registration and standards of care in residential accommodation for older people. The Centre for Policy on Ageing drew up the code which is based on optimal, rather than minimum standards.
c/f Residential care

Home Support

c/f Community-based services for elderly people

Home Visit

is a meeting with a client which takes place in their home, as contrasted with office based meetings. The home visit is preferred in specific circumstances, for example, where the office is inaccessible for some clients; where there is a need to meet on the client's own territory; when it can help reduce a client's social isolation (for the ill or housebound); where it can assist in the assessment of needs.
c/f Needs assessment

Homeless/Homelessness

People and families who have no accommodation or who are threatened with homelessness can apply to the local authority for re-housing. If they have dependant children, include a pregnant woman, are *vulnerable* because of old age, mental illness or disability, or have become homeless through an emergency or disaster, they are regarded as being in *priority need* under the 1985 Housing Act.

Authorities have a duty to provide accommodation for applicants in priority need categories, but only if their homelessness is unintentional. Single people are only regarded as being in priority need if they are childless, battered women and young homeless at risk of sexual or financial exploitation. Many other vulnerable people are homeless, including many who have spent much of their lives in institutions, children's homes, prisons, psychiatric hospitals, and so forth. Shelter and other voluntary agencies campaign for better treatment and services for homeless people, especially single homeless. The problem of homelessness is particularly acute in London and other major cities, where sleeping rough is increasingly common. Hostels, night shelters and resettlement units cater for an increasing number of people who are homeless and rootless.
c/f Night shelters/Points system/Resettlement units

Homesteading

c/f Estate action

Hospices

These are usually non-hospital buildings for the care and comfort of terminally ill people. They aim to provide as much of a homely atmosphere as possible and normally encourage friends and relatives to visit. In the UK the hospice movement has developed significantly in the last twenty years, particularly through voluntary effort. Many hospices also offer support for terminally ill people and their carers who are in their own homes.
c/f Bereavement/Terminally ill

Hostels

exist in many parts of the UK to provide accommodation for people living temporarily in an area, students and homeless people. The YMCA and YWCA hostels are amongst the best known, but over 50,000 bed spaces exist nationally, some catering for the poorest and most vulnerable, whilst others exist for categories such as overseas students and nurses.
c/f Homeless

Housing Action Trusts (HATs)

were established as a result of the 1988 Housing Act and were intended to take over the management of large, problematic council estates from local authorities. Some HATs have been established, but many have been opposed under the tenant's choice voting procedure. Part of the function of the HATs – and a controversial part – has been to divide up housing stock for disposal to other private landlords.
c/f Estate action/Priority estates project/Social housing/Tenant's choice/Voluntary transfer

Housing Association Grant (HAG)

This is the grant first established in 1974 and administered through the Housing Corporation, Tai Cymru and Scottish Homes for new housing developments. HAG is also paid through local authorities, though few new-build housing initiatives are taking place in the 1990s.
c/f Housing associations/Housing corporations

Housing Associations

The majority of new social housing in the UK is being built by
housing associations, funded by the government through the
Housing Corporation. Housing associations have a very long
history including the almshouses and large scale housing schemes
developed by charitable trusts such as Peabody and Guinness.
Rapid development of the voluntary housing sector in the 1980s
and early 1990s, under the direction of the Housing Corporation has
meant that well over a million people are now tenants of housing
associations. These all manage accommodation, which may be
converted, newly-built or transferred stock from local authorities.

Many housing associations offer rented accommodation aimed at
meeting the housing needs of particular groups such as elderly and
disabled people, homeless and single parents. Tenants in housing
associations usually have similar but not quite as extensive rights of
tenure and protection as local authority tenants.
c/f Almshouses/Housing corporation/Social housing

Housing Benefit

is the means-tested subsidy paid to individuals to enable them to
meet their rented accommodation costs. The government policy in
the late 1980s and early 1990s has been to use housing benefit to
make housing affordable for those on low incomes. Unfortunately,
the fact that rents have risen faster than inflation since 1979 means
that more and more tenants are caught in the *poverty trap* and are
unable to find income levels which allow them to move out of the
benefit system or increase their disposable income. Housing benefit
was first established under the Social Security and Housing Benefit
Act 1982.
c/f Affordability/Poverty trap/Social housing

Housing Co-operatives

do not have a single legally defined constitution and their
organisational structure varies throughout the UK. Confusingly, some
housing associations are also called co-ops, particularly community-
based housing associations. Mutual ownership or tenancy by
members of property owned or managed by the housing co-op is

Housing Co-operatives

a common feature of many co-ops. Par-value (meaning nominal financial stake in) co-ops and co-ownership, where all occupiers are buying a stake in their properties, are two major types. Scotland has developed the housing co-op as a form of co or community ownership and mutual tenancy to a greater degree than in England, but by and large co-operatives in the housing field have developed slowly in Britain as compared with many other countries in the world, especially in Norway and Sweden.
c/f Housing associations

Housing Corporation

This acts as the registration and supervisory agency for all 2,400 registered housing associations in England. Its role is increasingly important in providing affordable housing for families in need. The voluntary transfer of social housing stock from local authorities to housing associations and the establishment of the Tenant's Guarantee scheme for tenants in housing association accommodation has rapidly extended the power and influence of the Housing Corporation, which is based in London's Tottenham Court Road. It is usually referred to as a government quango and it channels government financial support to housing associations in England. It is controlled by a Board appointed by the Secretary of State for the Environment.
c/f Affordability/Housing associations/Scottish Homes/Social housing/Tai-Cymru/Tenant's guarantee/Voluntary transfer

I

Ice-breakers

These are types of games, exercises and sequences used in training and workshop sessions to promote involvement and activity, and to break down the inhibitions of participants.

Identification

is a psychological concept referring to the extent to which one person identifies with another. Identification is thought to be especially significant as a child develops and identifies with parents, other adults and peers as role models. Over identification with role models can create problematic behaviour for some people, and also poses problems of dependency.
c/f Dependency

Ideology

Any complex, but coherent system of ideas, political, religious, philosophical and so on, can be termed an ideology. Social work ideology is not entirely specific, but is often referred to obliquely. Amongst the ideological assumptions of most social welfare work is the view that society should become more just, equal and equitable in how wealth and resources are distributed. Generally, the more politicised and campaigning organisations and staff use the concept of 'ideology' as a synonym for having a clear belief system.

In Care

Being looked after in care is the result of the failure of the parents or guardians to provide 'suitable accommodation or care' and where the child is defined as 'in need' under section 20 of the Children Act 1989.
c/f Care/Care management/Child care/Leaving care/Looked after

Inadmissibility
c/f Admissibility

Income Support (IS)

is a state benefit paid to claimants who are *not* working for more than 16 hours per week and are regarded as having insufficient income on which to live. IS replaced supplementary benefit in 1988. It is regulated through the Social Security Act 1986 and the Income Support (General) Regulations 1987.
c/f Family Credit/Housing benefit

Independent Living

Programmes designed to help people live independently from social welfare support, or institutional and residential care are commonly called independent living programmes. Examples include establishing social and medical support and converting building environments to allow people with physical or mental disabilities to remain in their community. The Independent Living Fund has been established by the government as a result of Community Care legislation. It is designed to provide resources for people with disabilities to help them live independently.
c/f Community Care/Dependency/Disability/Normalisation

Individualisation

is one of the core social welfare principles, by which clients should expect to be treated as unique individuals. It implies clients as people, rather than group members, and may be part of a process of helping people to understand themselves.
c/f Empowerment/Self-actualisation

Individuation

Children develop their own identities and personalities through a process often called individuation. For example, as toddlers become independent from their mothers, this self-awareness is individuation.

Information Technology (IT)

is the umbrella term covering the range of computer applications used to store and organise information. The use of computers in social welfare has expanded rapidly and presently covers administration; secretarial; record-keeping; monitoring and evaluation;

Information Technology (IT)

financial budgets. In turn, these stores of information can inform planning, management and practice if used in informed and constructive ways.

Confusingly, the initials IT are also used for Intermediate Treatment, and outside of the social welfare world, Intermediate Technology.

c/f Data protection/Intermediate treatment/Recording

Inherent Jurisdiction

In the 1970s and 1980s, local authorities used the power of the High Court to make an increasing number of children wards of court. The judges had this power under the High Court's ancient non-statutory rights over children, which are referred to in legal parlance as their 'inherent jurisdiction'. This power has been restricted by the Children Act 1989 to cases where the local authorities are unable for some reason to use statutory procedures such as a care order or supervision order.

c/f Care Order/Supervision Order/Wardship

In-house Training

c/f In-service training

Inquorate

c/f Quorum

In-service Training

covers the training requirements and opportunities offered by an organisation or professional service. Most social welfare organisations offer at least some training which is most likely to be organised 'in-house'. *Induction training* is introductory training; *basic training* is used to describe training in basic skills, competences and procedures; *specialist training opportunities* tend to reflect responses to changes in legislation, responsibilities and the individual training needs of staff members.

Social Welfare agencies are expected to make use of the National Vocational Qualification Social Care competences for training staff

In-service Training (cont'd)

in basic and more advanced skills. Other specialist areas, such as youth work and community work, are also developing curricula under the aegis of the NVQ system.
c/f Competence/National Vocational Qualifications

Institutionalisation

is the sum total of the negative effects for individuals living in institutional environments: residential care, prisons, Young Offender Institutions and for some, even the armed forces and public schools. The effects of institutionalisation are to restrict liberty, stultify individual thinking and behaviour, and make it difficult for people who have been in institutions to cope with society outside of their limited environment.
c/f Institutions/Normalisation/Residential care

Institutions

There are two meanings of 'institution'. The first relates to organisations and particularly the buildings used by them to offer services and facilities. The term has a negative implication for many institutions are believed to exist to punish, treat or alter the individual. Prison, residential care and services offered for clients with special needs can restrict freedom of choice and lead to a conditional dependency known as *institutionalisation*.

In the wider sense, *education* and *social welfare* themselves are considered institutions meaning *total social systems*. Forms of socially acceptable behaviour such as *marriage* are also referred to as institutions.
c/f Normalisation/Residential care

Intake

refers to the initial response made by social work agencies.
Some social work agencies employ special Intake Teams. Their responsibilities vary between agencies, but most: offer information about available resources; provide an initial assessment of need; assign or refer the client to a suitable worker or service. In social

Intake

work terms, they act as gate-keepers to prevent inappropriate admission to services, and act as the first level referral agency. Intake teams were popular in the 1980s, but have declined since.
c/f Assessment/Gate-keeping/Referral

Interactive

Being interactive is the process of exchanging information and ideas. In social welfare, certain training techniques, research and investigative tests and learning aids are deemed interactive because they encourage interaction between people. A number of videos, CDs and computer software and audio cassettes are on the market under the broad title of 'interactive'. Most solicit responses and allow the user(s) to get involved in the process of use by answering questions, making choices and selecting options.
c/f Information technology/Proactive/Reactive

Inter-agency

c/f Multi-agency/Multi-disciplinary

Inter-disciplinary Agency

c/f Multi-agency/Multi-disciplinary

Interface

Interface is the point of meeting or joining together of two separate organisations or systems. In welfare, this computer term is used for how two or more organisational systems can effectively work together.
c/f Hardware/Software

Intermediate Treatment (IT)

is a term which came from the 1968 White Paper *Children in Trouble* where a new provision of programmes for juvenile offenders 'intermediate' between individual social work supervision and residential care was proposed. The 1969 Children and Young

Intermediate Treatment (IT) (cont'd)

Persons Act and section 20 of the 1982 Criminal Justice Act have underpinned what IT in England and Wales consists of, moving from social groupwork including many recreational activities to more structured intensive IT programmes designed to modify juveniles' offending behaviour. IT groups are usually run by social work staff, sometimes with voluntary help. Funding has come from central government funds, Urban Aid and from local authorities and voluntary agencies. The DHSS IT programme helped to reduce the annual population of Young Offenders' Institutions from 7,500 in 1984 to approximately 2,000 in 1990.

The Scottish IT system has developed differently from the English partly because of the existence of the Children's Hearing system. The Scottish IT groups have historically been more focused on preventative welfare work, whilst England has developed IT more as a direct alternative to custody.
c/f Juvenile justice/Juvenile offenders

Intervention

Intervention means taking action. Each intervention can vary considerably ranging from advocacy, information, treatment, counselling, groupwork to therapy and medical care. The main problem in social welfare work is choosing the nature and level of an intervention, and judging whether that intervention is accepted or resented by the recipient.
c/f Counselling/Treatment

Interview

Social welfare interviews are organised for a variety of reasons. Individuals, couples, families and groups may all be interviewed as part of a fact and information gathering exercise; as a means of problem-solving; for a formal needs assessment; or as a method of counselling. The relationship between interviewer and interviewees will vary depending upon the reason behind a particular interview, and the power position of each participant.

An interview schedule is a formal research survey tool for gathering information through the use of open or closed-ended questions.
c/f Assessment/Counselling/Directive/Non-directive

Inventory

An inventory is a specific type of interview schedule used in social research. The inventory is used to evaluate the presence or absence of particular occurrences, attitudes or behaviour.

c/f Interview/Research

J

Jobcentre

Provided through the Employment Service, jobcentres are the local centres for the display of job vacancies. The jobcentre acts as a job-broker, working with employers and those seeking work. Many jobcentres have specialist provision for certain trades and careers, such as catering and building, and other specialist services are operated nationally (such as job opportunities for nurses and the Professional and Executive Register).
c/f Disablement resettlement officers/Employment service/Gateway

Judicial Process

describes all that happens in courts and also other legal processes, such as tribunals, which can involve social welfare staff in Mental Health Review Tribunals, Industrial Tribunals and Registered Home Tribunals.
c/f Courts

Justice/Justice System

The terms 'justice system' and 'justice' relate to the activities carried out by all the social organisations which deal with offenders: courts, police, legal profession, judiciary, prisons, probation and social work. Some social workers and probation staff would not include themselves in the justice system, but this is probably a naive view.

Justice system is also used to describe the system of proportionality, where sentencing relates directly to the offence, as opposed to a welfare approach which looks to provide the most appropriate response to individual offenders.
c/f Courts/Proportionality/Tariff system/Welfare system

Juvenile

A juvenile, in the eyes of the law, is a young person aged between fourteen and seventeen years old.

Juvenile Courts
c/f Youth courts

Juvenile Delinquency
as a term is less fashionable than in the 1950s and 1960s. Delinquent is synonymous with young offender. Juvenile delinquency encompasses any anti-social and criminal activity, ranging from breaking a pane of glass in a telephone box to grievous bodily harm. *c/f Youth court*

Juvenile Liaison
The police force has a special section for working with young people. This is known as the Juvenile Liaison Service. Officers undergo special training both in terms of face-to-face work with children and juveniles, and on aspects of legislation concerning this age group and on the particular responsibilities of the police in respect of court work, probation and specialist areas such as child abuse and child protection.

K

Keep the Peace

c/f Bound-over

Keyworker/Keyworking

In social welfare work, the role of keyworker and the activity of keyworking have both very specific *AND* general meaning. The keyworker role does not necessarily imply qualification, but the Social Care Association (among others) have suggested that a keyworker is the person primarily accountable for a particular service user. Keyworking as an activity will then include ensuring quality of service; evolving a care plan; making recommendations; monitoring progress and keeping records. The keyworker is usually the person who maintains most regular contact with a service user, and in community care should ensure that the wishes of a person are fully respected and that users are consulted and offered choices.
c/f Community care/Networking

Knowledge Base

The ideology ethos or philosophy of social welfare is sometimes referred to as the knowledge base. Social work as a professional discipline is based on the social or human sciences and uses the theoretical knowledge base of psychology, sociology and occasionally psychiatry.

K

Keep the Pace

Keyword/Keywords

Knowledge Base

L

Labelling

is the name given to the process whereby a person or their problem places them in a social category. In social work, labels are frequently assigned to behaviour which is seen to be deviant from social norms. In this way, labelling a particular activity as an 'offence' creates a pattern of behaviour categorised as 'offending behaviour' by offenders. Becoming labelled as a social work 'client' or 'patient' or 'mentally ill' can have adverse effects on the treatment an individual receives, and research studies, in particular by Howard Becker in America, have shown how labels can become self-fulfilling prophesies and a form of discrimination.

However, in certain cases, labelling can also fulfil a positive function. For instance, labelling a person as requiring special educational provision based on needs will produce a positive service response for that person. This is particularly the case, for instance, with autistic people, who will not receive services unless their condition is 'officially' recognised.

c/f Discrimination/Gate-keeping

Latchkey Children

During school holidays and in the hours after school, many parents find it difficult to provide adequate arrangements for looking after their children. This is particularly the case for some single parents and parents who work. Children are then left either with a key to an empty house or with nowhere to go except the street until their parent(s) return. This has led to them being referred to as latchkey children. The Children Act 1989 placed the responsibility for providing out-of-school facilities for under-eights 'in need' on the local authority social services, but the development of these services is hampered by limited resources.

c/f Out-of-school clubs/Playcare

Learning Difficulty/Disability

has become the generally preferred term to replace mental handicap. It covers the entire range of disabilities which cause individuals to intellectually function below average, or have difficulties with adaptive behaviour. This includes specific learning difficulties such as dyslexia, but can also apply to the whole range of mental disabilities.
c/f Disability/Mental handicap/Mental health/Normalisation/ Vulnerable people

Learning Styles

This concept is associated with adult learning theory, which suggests that each person learns in a particular way. According to Kolb and associates, there are four major styles that interact with one another to form an individual's own style. These refer to learning by: a) doing or action, b) critical reflection and evaluation, c) use of concepts and theories, d) planning and preparation for action. In reality, most people use a mixture of the four styles of learning.

Social welfare staff frequently need to use an analysis of how individuals learn in order to try and offer advice, assistance or development of care or treatment plans. Different people receive stimulation or are put off learning because they do not 'learn' in homogenous ways. Treatment plans based on the psychological system known as *behaviour modification* use an assessment of learning styles to understand fears, problems and strengths. These are especially helpful in enabling the development of *experiential learning*, where individuals are encouraged to reflect on their own experience and behaviour and to investigate and manage change.
c/f Behaviour modification/Experiential learning/Personal constructs/ Psychology

Leaving Care

After the age of sixteen, children in care (voluntary) under section 20 of the Children Act 1989, can discharge themselves. Local authorities still have discretionary powers to provide accommodation until twenty-one-years of age. The problems faced by many youngsters leaving care include: lack of ongoing financial and material support; inadequate preparation for independent living; insufficient emotional support.

Leaving Care

Section 24 of the Children Act imposes a duty on local authorities to *advise* and *befriend* persons under twenty one who have spent any time after their sixteenth birthday in accommodation under the Act. There may also be assistance given for young people leaving care for accommodation, employment, education and training. The Children Act also recommends closer liaison between social services and housing departments.
c/f Care/In care/Looked after

Licensees

Adult prisoners, aged 18 or over, serving sentences of more than twelve months, and most young offenders, regardless of length of their sentence are subject to supervision on release. Probation officers under the Probation Service National Standards (1992) are charged with the supervision of ex-offenders who are termed 'licensees'.

Increasingly, licensees see the post-release supervision as part of the 'punishment' and since many have spent at least some of their childhood in institutional care and have a history of mental illness, there is increasing pressure on probation officers.
c/f Breach proceedings/Probation and after care service

Listening Skills

Social welfare staff are frequently expected to have good listening skills. These require *empathy* – perception of, and understanding and sympathy for the person to whom they are listening – and *cognitive ability* – understanding, remembering and evaluation of information received.
c/f Counselling/Empathy

Logs

are a form of written record used to keep track of relatively straightforward information such as attendance, staffing levels, expenditure. They are used for simple administrative recording of social work tasks and performance. A more elaborate form of log is a 'diary', which can be used professionally to record behaviour, observations, lessons learned, and so on.
c/f Assessment/Evaluation/Monitoring/Recording

Looked after/Looking after

This common language expression has taken on special meaning for residential care staff, since it is being used as a synonymous term to 'in care'. Therefore, although 'looking after children or young people in care' is frequently used, 'looking after' on its own implies being in care.

c/f Care/Care Order

Loss/Loss Situations

Loss is a common human experience, but it can be extremely difficult to come to terms with it. Feelings of guilt and suppression of an emotional response are two typical reactions. A sense of loss can arise as a result of: relationship break up – divorce and separation; physical or mental loss – disability, senility, impairment; economic loss – through unemployment, eviction, homelessness; failed achievement – not obtaining exam passes, childlessness, rejection after an interview for a new job.

Many welfare staff in health and social settings try to assist individuals with coping with loss and grief. The terminally ill, AIDs sufferers, young people in loss situations, widows and widowers, survivors of tragedies and their relatives, all may require support from informal or formal counsellors. Aids such as trigger-pictures, writing a diary, family trees, drawing a picture and looking at photographs are all used by counsellors, but listening and empathy are probably the most important skills in loss situations. Additionally, it is important for counsellors to receive their own support and supervision because of the stressful nature of grief.

c/f Bereavement

M

Mainlining

In addition to the street drug culture expression for injecting drugs, mainlining is also used in welfare organisations to describe projects or organisations which become directly, and normally permanently, funded by local or central government.

Management Information System (MIS)

A Management Information System provides a computer-based system for storing and organising information. A system suitable for social welfare work requires each part of that system to be integrated (linked) to each other part. It can be used to track the career of clients while in contact with an agency and the eventual outcomes of interventions.
c/f Information technology

Mandatory Legislation

Local authorities have duties imposed on them through mandatory legislation, but even then the term used may be very general and leave local authorities with wide discretion as to how services should be organised, and what level of service to provide. For instance, local housing authorities, under the 1985 Housing Act must offer help to homeless people in 'priority need', but it is left to the local authorities to assess need and to decide whether a homeless person has become intentionally homeless or not.
c/f Discretion/Permissive legislation

Mapping

is a technique used in evaluation exercises to assess what is actually happening in a service or to a service user. In a geographical area a social work or community work team might wish to find out what community resources exist and what they provide. The collection and collation of this information is known as mapping. The same term is

Mapping (cont'd)

often used for tracking what happens to a client, for example, referral – assessment – service options or no further action.
c/f Evaluation/Profiling

Marriage

The break up of marriages and partnerships creates a large amount of work for social welfare agencies. Marriage and personal relationship counselling occupies a vast amount of voluntary agency time for organisations such as Relate and the Catholic Marriage Advisory Council. Youth workers, teachers and some youth social workers also get actively involved in social education with children and young people so that marriage and living together are carefully considered before young people team up. Conciliation work involves probation and social work staff in assisting couples deal with relationship difficulties and the practical problems of maintenance and access.
c/f Conciliation/Counselling/Divorce/Relate

Meals-on-wheels

This local authority service for elderly people in their own homes is frequently provided through the Women's Royal Voluntary Service and the British Red Cross Society. Local authority policies on price and eligibility for the service vary considerably.
c/f Community based services for elderly people/Domiciliary care

Means Testing

is applied in assessing eligibility for benefits. These are usually non-contributory benefits (i.e. not linked to National Insurance contributions). Individuals need to include their savings, income and also their special needs, as single parents, disabled, and so on.
c/f Social security

Mediation

has both a technical, specific meaning and a more general use. Mediation schemes have been established in some areas of the UK in working with offenders and victims. These schemes have two-fold

Mediation

aims: to give victims an active opportunity to see that justice has been done, and to give offenders a chance to make good for their criminal activity.

Mediation is also used to describe activities undertaken by welfare staff where they act as conciliators or go-betweens in cases of dispute such as matrimonial proceedings.
c/f Reparation/Victim support

Mental Disorders

In psychiatry, this term is used to refer to three groups of mental disorder, namely psychoses, neurotic disorders and mental impairment. Mental illness and mental disorders are sometimes used synonymously. The 1983 Mental Health Act defined 'mental disorder' as including mental illness, arrested or incomplete development of the mind, psychopathic disorder, other disorders or disabilities of the mind.
c/f Disability/Mental ill health/Mental impairment

Mental Handicap

In the 1970s, the term mental handicap replaced mental subnormality. It has now largely been replaced by learning difficulty or disability as the preferred term.
c/f Learning difficulty/Vulnerable people

Mental Health

is usually used to describe the positive functions of people at an emotional and psychological level. Mental health implies the ability to cope with environmental and social pressures, and internal conflict. It also indicates a state of stability and personal performance, which allows an individual to experience satisfaction and fulfilment.
c/f Mental ill health

Mental Health Teams

Teams of multi-disciplinary staff frequently work together in the treatment of mental disorders, mental ill health and learning disabilities. Sometimes they are employed by a single agency, in

Mental Health Teams (cont'd)

other instances, they collaborate to offer support for vulnerable people. Mental health teams may include clinical psychologists, psychiatrists, psychiatric nurses, occupational therapists, social workers and doctors.

c/f Community mental health teams/Community teams for people with learning difficulties/Multi-disciplinary/Normalisation/Vulnerable people

Mental Ill Health

is now preferred to mental illness as a term to describe impaired functioning by disturbance in thinking, doing or feeling. The severity of mental ill health is extremely variable and the causes are equally complex, including biological, chemical, physiological, genetic, social, familial, and psychological malfunction.

The treatment of illnesses associated with mental ill health, usually require specific medical responses. However, the support of people experiencing mental health problems, for instance with accommodation, skills training and cultural and recreational activities *are* the responsibility of social care staff.

c/f Learning difficulties/Mental disorders/Mental health

Mental Illness

There is no clear definition of what is and what is not a mental illness. The Mental Health Act 1983 fails to define mental illness, but does offer a range of definitions for candidates described as severe and significant *mental impairment*.

Mental illness is frequently used to describe all mental conditions which require treatment. Schizophrenia, neuroses, personality and psychosexual disorders and psychoses are examples of conditions regarded as mental illness.

c/f Mental disorders/Mental ill health/Mental impairment

Mental Impairment

has replaced mental retardation as the term used for people suffering from 'a state of arrested or incomplete development of the mind which includes severe or significant impairment of intelligence or social functioning' (paraphrased from the Mental Health Act 1983).

Mental Impairment

Approaches to mental impairment increasingly involve inter-disciplinary, multi-agency work. Social care staff are particularly important in co-ordinating assistance, and in helping empower vulnerable people to be more independent and self-determining, as far as is practicable.
c/f Mental disorders/Mental health/Mental illness

Milieu Therapy

is a specific form of treatment or therapy usually employed in residential care settings with socially or mentally disordered people. Everyone in the institutional group becomes a part of a closed community, which may also be referred to as a therapeutic community. Within this group they elect their own leaders and provide a mutual social support. The environment or milieu is considered part of the treatment or therapeutic process.
c/f Residential care/Therapy/Token economy

Mission Statement

is the term used to describe the core values of an organisation or team. In social care, the elements usually include 'best' care for consumers; value for money; performance improvement and monitoring; quality and training for staff; empowerment and partnership strategies for consumers. It will relate to more specifically targetted aims and goals for the organisational unit. It has been suggested that a mission statement should consist of a single statement, which distils the essence of an organisation's purpose and activities.

Mobile Assessment Teams

These are the thirty mobile teams who provide an assessment for people with disabilities. They offer support and advice particularly in relation to employment and training opportunities.
c/f ACTs/ASSET centres/Employment Rehabilitation Service

Modelling

In social learning theory, modelling is imitative behaviour. The term is more often used to describe negative learning, such as learning

Modelling (cont'd)

anxiety, fear or dislike of something. Staff (and parents!) with children, will frequently see a particular child 'model' their response to a situation by copying a peer, saying: "I don't like vegetables" or "I'm afraid of the dentist".
c/f Groupwork

Monitoring

is usually regarded as part of the larger process of evaluation. Monitoring involves collecting information based on some pre-determined set of criteria. A questionnaire is one of the simpler ways in which data and views can be collected. Consumer views are increasingly important as the social welfare services are steered towards being market-led. Likewise, the nature of services received, the perceived quality of services and the performance of staff (competences) can all be monitored, which is a first step towards assessment and evaluation.
c/f Competence/Evaluation/Questionnaire

Multi-agency

describes active collaboration by a number of agencies or departments of local or central government working together for a common aim or goal. Usually in social welfare, these multi-agency agreements formalise informal networks which may already have existed. They were originally referred to as inter-agency working, but 'multi-agency' is now the current terminology and implies a more complex and comprehensive approach. Examples of multi-agency work can involve strategic planning; management and co-ordination; service delivery and evaluation and monitoring. Therefore, in speaking of a multi-agency *approach*, it is describing a form of *systems organisation* and a *method* of working. Many multi-agency collaborations, as in child protection work, involve a mixture of statutory and voluntary agencies, such as Health, Social Services and Education departments, their specialist staff, police, and agencies such as the NSPCC.
c/f Multi-disciplinary/Networking

Multi-disciplinary

indicates that a group of professional staff from different disciplines, who have undertaken different forms of professional training are working together in a team of staff, or a less formal network. Social welfare encourages multi-disciplinary work, where particular client groups such as children or young people can benefit from collaborative inputs from a variety of professions. Some professional rivalry and distrust can still exist even where departments and agencies have agreed to work in multi-disciplinary organisational ways. However, the professions are being forced by new legislation such as the 1989 Children Act, Mental Health Act 1983 and the NHS and Community Care Act 1990 to work in more integrated ways. *c/f Multi-agency/Networking*

N

National Health Service (NHS)

The NHS is administered by the Secretary of State for Health, and the Secretaries of State for Wales and Scotland. It was established under the NHS Act 1946 and amended under the NHS Act 1977 and the NHS and Community Care Act 1990. The establishment of GP practices as fund-holders, contracting for purchasing of services and the setting up of NHS Trusts, has brought into question how far the NHS is a system of universally available provision. The NHS is still mostly free or on a subsidised basis and includes hospital, GP, and dental services, drugs, spectacles and contact lenses.
c/f Community Care/Welfare state

National Vocational Qualifications (NVQs)

have come to the forefront of training policy in the current world of social welfare. The Care Sector Consortium established the structure and content for the first awards which are at levels II and III, but there are also plans for level I and level IV awards which follow the pattern of integrating health and social care. It is proposed that the Diploma in Social Work will be the equivalent of level IV, which may become the attainment level generally for professional qualifications, for instance, in nursing, teaching, social welfare.

The NVQ is a qualification which is proof of competence that a candidate has been assessed as performing to the required standard. The NVQ award is accredited by the National Council for Vocational Qualifications. As the system grows, more and more specialist NVQs will come on stream.

The NVQ process takes account of a candidate's past experience and qualifications, current evidence of knowledge application and performance and evidence from interviews and observation in the work-based assessment.
c/f Accreditation of prior learning/Competence/Critical enabling knowledge/Performance criteria

Naturalisation

is being suggested by some people with disabilities as a better term for the process of 'normalisation'. The argument is that handicaps and disabilities are normal or natural, and that empowerment to overcome disabilities and learning difficulties is a process of naturalisation.

The more common, everyday use of naturalisation is 'to become a citizen of a country'.

c/f Normalisation

Needs Assessment

is a process which is designed to look at both the means and circumstances of a family or an individual, relative to what is regarded as 'normal' in that community. The assessment stage makes an estimate of what action and resources are required to assist that family or person, depending upon perceived urgency of their need.

Neighbourhood Work

Many writers and staff see community work and neighbourhood work as synonymous. In social work, neighbourhood work usually means utilising the flexible, formal and informal networks which exist in communities. The boundary of any 'neighbourhood' may be hard to draw, but the concepts of *belonging* and *territory* are frequently the everyday, shared notions which underlie social relations in an area. Neighbourhood work may include assisting people to help each other; achieve changes; represent themselves to authorities; receive improved services. Community care, with its focus on empowerment, is a further development of the principle that social welfare should go local and be more accountable to the communities being served.

c/f Community development/Community work/Patchwork

Net-widening

is a term used to describe the process whereby consumers of social welfare services are processed by the social services organisations in ways which inappropriately 'label' them through that intervention. This can have the effect of stigmatising the recipient of the service

Net-widening

and moving them on to more intensive services more quickly
than should be the case. Put simply, net-widening creates clients
and categorises them as problems when a more creative systems
intervention is to avoid formal processing unless it is absolutely
necessary.
c/f Labelling/Systems intervention

Networking

is usually used to describe a social work method or process which
allows and extends access to resources. These networks can be
people, organisations, services, skills, information and buildings.
Networking involves putting people in touch with one another in
creative partnerships. These *communities of partnership* may be
between service users and social welfare staff or within staff groups
or user groups. Examples would include many tenant participation
and housing association groups which make contact with and use
formal and *informal* social networks to improve co-operation and
communication.
c/f Action-sets/Community care/Empowerment/Facilitation

Neurolinguistic Programming (NLP)

is a communications system which allows practitioners to identify
and empathise with a client's view of the world. It does this through
identifying the *neuro* – information received through the five senses;
the *linguistic* – messages communicated verbally and non-verbally,
and *programming* – which enables individuals to identify and control
outcomes more effectively. It is increasingly used by social work and
counselling staff.

New Client Advisors

In the Employment Service, New Client Advisors are the staff who
advise new claimants about job search, training and enterprise
opportunities. They check eligibility to claim benefit, and, if
appropriate, help their clients to work out a back-to-work plan and
look at existing vacancies.
c/f Employment service

Night Shelters

are the name used for emergency accommodation projects providing beds and food for single homeless people. Agencies such as St. Mungo's Community Trust and the Salvation Army provide baseline assistance and support for many of the most vulnerable homeless.
c/f Homeless

Non-accidental Injury

This is the relatively neutral term, which is now less frequently used to describe physical and sexual abuse in children cases. The Maria Colwell report (HMSO 1974) was one of the most influential cases in social work and led to far greater attention being given to early intervention in suspected cases of child abuse and neglect, and more use of the children at risk register, now called the *child protection register*.
c/f Child protection/Child sexual abuse/Family violence

Non-directive

This term seems to have been used most in relation to the style and method of face-to-face work undertaken in neighbourhood *detached work* with young people. Non-directive work implies a worker providing a non-judgemental adult presence, a very loose support structure of advice, information and counselling. Much non-directive work is undertaken in difficult and sometimes threatening social situations such as pubs, street corners and cafes where the worker is on the territory of the young person. The non-directive approach has also spilled over into counselling, therapy and drugs work, where workers frequently try to help people to help themselves.
c/f Counselling/Detached youth work/Directive

Normalisation

refers to the principles of ordinary living, which have been adopted as a main aim of Community Care, particularly in relation to people with learning difficulties or special needs. Normalisation principles are based on people with special needs being able to lead ordinary lives in ordinary places, where they can make choices and social

Normalisation

contacts, acquire skills and be respected and accepted for what they are. Normalisation implies adopting strategies, through formal and informal intervention, to help people as far as possible look after themselves and live independent lives outside of institutions.
c/f Community care/Institutionalisation/Residential care

Nuclear Family

The classic nuclear family is made up of mother, father and their children. As divorce and separation have increased, a wider variety of family groups and households have formed and gay couples, communities and institutional residential care all provide alternative models of family care.
c/f Extended family/Family

Nursery

Day care services in nurseries for children below school age are required to register with the local authority and are subject to inspection. In many authorities the local education department provides some nursery school education for children between two and five years old. This is also known as pre-school provision.
c/f Child minders/Creche

Nursing Homes for Elderly People

Nursing Homes are registered with the Health Authority, and the person in charge must be a registered medical practitioner or registered nurse. Nursing Homes, like Residential Care Homes, are registered under the provisions of the 1984 Registered Homes Act.

In general terms, Nursing Homes cater for people who are actually ill, receive regular medical attention in every 24 hours, and need more nursing help than can be offered in their own homes or in residential care homes. In the past fifteen years, there has been a shift in the criteria of admission of elderly people into both care homes and nursing homes. Many people who would previously have been cared for in hospital are now cared for in nursing homes.
c/f Residential care homes

O

Obligation

Local authorities are obliged to make available a wide range of services. The specific services are covered under legislation which can include a mixture of services from social services, health and housing authorities. The obligation to provide housing for single homeless people is an example, albeit a complicated one. The 1985 Housing Act obliges local authorities to make accommodation available for single people only if they are in priority need, which includes vulnerable young people, pregnant women and women with children. However, the obligation may be rescinded if the applicant is seen as being intentionally homeless, or the responsibility of another authority.
c/f Discretion

Occupational Standards Council

is the name of the successor to the Care Sector Consortium.
c/f Care Sector Consortium

Occupational Therapy/Therapists

is principally a service run by staff providing a range of advice on mobility, employment and age and disability related services. The therapy aspects include forms of physical treatment and counselling and group work programmes. Services can be directly provided by local authorities or contracted out to voluntary and private agencies.
c/f Vocational rehabilitation

Older People

Older people constitute an increasing proportion of the total population. This demographic change has put an additional responsibility and financial pressure on local authorities charged with providing support and facilities for older or elderly people. By 1992, it was estimated that approximately 40 per cent of gross services expenditure would be on services for older people. Broadly, these

Older People (cont'd)

services include a) *community-based services*: including payments
to help older people remain in their own homes; more help to carers;
increased day and community-based services; home helps, meals
service. b) *Residential services*: care homes, nursing homes and
integrated resource centres offering accommodation and a range of
care and support, including medical assistance. c) *Registration and
inspection services*: primarily aimed at ensuring minimum standards
in residential care in both private and statutory facilities. A quasi-
official guide to the provision of optimal standards in residential care
entitled *Home Life* was published by the Centre for Policy on Ageing.
Help the Aged and Age Concern provide information and advice on
all aspects of the welfare for older or elderly people.
*c/f Community-based services/Nursing homes/Residential care
homes*

On Licence

refers to people released from prisons or young offenders'
institutions, who are on parole, which means that they will be
supervised by the probation service until the expiry of their licence.
Non-compliance can result in return to prison or a Young Offenders'
Institution.
c/f After-care/Probation

Open Employment

is often used to describe the aim of vocational guidance and
rehabilitation work with people with a range of learning disabilities.
Open employment is work obtained in the open market, not through
special employment schemes.
c/f Normalisation/Vocational Rehabilitation

Open Groups

These are groups which allow for changing and variable membership
during the course of their life. In social work, they are types
of specialised, structured groups operated in group work and
therapeutic settings. Frequently they are viewed as 'open' by virtue
of open access for participants who can join the group (or leave the

Open Groups

group) freely, or at particular times. However, like closed groups, they will usually have set inclusion criteria. They are used in child protection work with survivors; intermediate treatment work with young offenders and in a variety of other contexts including family groups, drugs work and mental health work. Participants may agree to set the boundaries and rules for membership and participation and these can be embodied in a contract with the facilitator.
c/f Boundary maintenance/Closed groups/Contracts/Groupwork/ Safeguards

Open Learning

is a term increasingly used in training to describe courses and modules of staff training which are flexibly organised to take account of an individual's experience, and use that experience as a basis for learning. Much 'open learning' is organised through a mixture of self-programmed learning at a distance from any supervision, coupled with the use of specially designed materials which link the learning to particular course frameworks. Open learning may be assessed, as may other courses of study, and it can also be linked to the NVQ system.
c/f Distance learning/Experiential learning/National Vocational Qualifications

Orange Book

The Orange Book is one of the social worker's 'bibles'. The full and proper name is *Protecting Children: A guide for social workers undertaking a comprehensive assessment*, and it is used as the basis for local authority social work applications in court.
c/f Assessment/Child protection

Outcomes

In everyday language, an outcome is the result of interventions and events. In social welfare, workers, managers and planners are always working to refine the predictability of outcomes, so that interventions can be made which produce a higher degree of successful, positive outcomes. Outcome research measures the result of changing the

Outcomes (cont'd)

ways in which services are organised or delivered. For instance, outcome research can be used to measure the frequency at which children taken into care return to their original homes and after what length of time. Providing a clear definition of 'outcomes' is, however, frequently problematic in many forms of social intervention, which in turn makes evaluation extremely difficult.
c/f Assessment/Evaluation/Monitoring/Research

Out-of-school Clubs

Clubs and facilities aimed at providing care and play for children after school and in school holidays are becoming more common in the wake of the Children Act 1989. The Act gave local authorities and social services departments the responsibility (and problem) of providing out of school care for children in need. Clubs and schemes have been slow to develop because of limited financial resources, but the Kids Club Network has been at the forefront of campaigning pressure groups to encourage new initiatives in this area, particularly in supporting parents to start self-help clubs.
c/f Latchkey children/Play/Play care

Outreach

is used to describe both a type of staff and a work approach. Staff who are employed to work in the community, rather than being based in a particular building are referred to as outreach workers. The term is used most frequently in youth service, welfare rights and adult education.
c/f Detached youth work

P

Paradigm

Academic writers describing social welfare functions have a
tendency to use 'paradigm' as a synonym for *an example* or *body of
knowledge.*
c/f Epistemology

Paraprofessional

Staff who work as assistants to professionally qualified colleagues in
social welfare, or in allied occupations and task groups, are known
as paraprofessionals. The term is also applied to individuals who take
over social work tasks after a period of training.

Parental Responsibility

has been established under the law by various pieces of legislation.
For social welfare staff, the 1989 Children Act is the key piece of
legislation which redefined parental rights as parental responsibility.
It was defined in the Act by Lord Mackay as "the responsibility for
caring and for raising the child to a properly developed adult both
physically and morally".

Under the law, the child's welfare is paramount, above the
interests or views of the parents, and this is central in all court
decision making. Social work intervention in families is ideally kept
to the minimum and the 1989 Act stated that social workers must
demonstrate a risk of 'significant harm' before local authority care is
considered.

Parental Rights

c/f Parental responsibility

Parole

c/f On-licence

Parsimony

is a principle or approach which means 'sparingly' or with economy. In work in the criminal justice system, parsimony is sometimes urged with regard to the use of custodial sentences, because many feel that penal institutions damage inmates rather than help reform them, and that custodial sentences do not act as a deterrent to further offending.
c/f Custodial sentences

Pastoral Care

is a form of counselling and support offered to children in some schools. Usually a teacher is designated as having responsibility for pastoral care in the school, but in some cases, form teachers take on this role for their class members. Pastoral care is used to describe all forms of support and counselling in non-school work. So, for instance, concern about behaviour (in general), suspected child abuse and matrimonial problems may all initially be dealt with through the school pastoral care system, but may be referred subsequently to other agencies.
c/f Child protection/Counselling/Social education

Patchwork

is a method of service delivery operated in some social services departments. It involves allocating cases to social workers on the basis of geographical distribution in 'patches', which are local areas, often with distinct community boundaries. The rationale behind 'patchwork' is to make social work more accessible and accountable to consumers. Social workers operating in a patch system may either be members of specialist teams or offering a generic, full range of social work services. To work effectively, patchwork and 'going local' entail professional social welfare staff becoming more involved in active partnerships and user-involvement in the development of community-based social services.
c/f Community care/Community development/Neighbourhood work/Social work

Pathologise

describes the process of classification and diagnostic labelling of social and behavioural problems, analagous to those in medicine from where the term is derived. Social welfare perspectives tend to oppose *disease models* which attribute the causes of social problems to individual weaknesses. Actions which 'pathologise' an offending, or criminal activity reinforce a *deviant label*, and make positive social work intervention more difficult. Pathological processes also tend to focus on the individual in terms of both diagnosis and treatment, thereby ignoring wider social factors and positive interventions.
c/f Behaviour modification/Labelling

Patient's Charter

This Charter was an application of the Conservative government's policy of regulating public services with reference to a user's rights to a service. The Patient's Charter focuses on improving standards of service, particularly with regard to the length of waiting lists for hospital treatment, and allowing patients greater choice of doctors and available services.

Critics have suggested that the Charter's main function is to allow the government to gradually privatise the National Health Service.
c/f Citizen's Charter/Citizenship

Patient Trail

c/f Client trail

Peer Counselling

is sometimes also referred to as co-counselling. It is a technique which can be used by two or more workers who share a similar professional background, are empathetic, and trust each other. The aim is to create mutual, critical support through using structured meetings, outlining problems and difficulties, and through offering constructive feedback to each other. The counsellor or listener(s) may offer comments and suggestions, but this is not always welcomed. The roles are then switched with another member of the

Peer Counselling (cont'd)

peer counselling group or pair describing a problem situation of their choice.
c/f Counselling/Co-working

Peer Group

is a group of individuals who are of a similar age or who have a similar social status or professional background. The term 'peer group' is often applied to friendship groups of young people, who may also be categorised as gangs, teams or members.

People with Learning Difficulties (PLD)

This group are synonymous with people with learning disabilities and include people with a range of mental handicaps.
c/f Learning difficulty/Vocational rehabilitation

People Work

'People work' is used by some writers and trainers as the umbrella term which embraces all the professions and organisations who work in the range of the personal social services: social work; education; housing; work with offenders and health.
c/f Personal social services/Social work

Performance Criteria

are determined by agencies in social welfare to ensure that standards of service delivery and quality are adhered to. Performance criteria are often used as the measure of competence of staff in performing tasks and keeping to the principles, values and ethics of professional practice. Usually they relate to *how* a task is being performed.
c/f Competence/Standards

Performance Indicators

These are often established to assess the overall performance of an organisation, by examining its component parts: service provision, service development, staffing, finance, buildings and facilities, equipment. Under each heading it is possible for social welfare

Performance Indicators

organisations to determine performance indicators such as regularity of inspection, number of cases per staff member, staff illness rates. These can all be measured and will help managers and policy-planners to determine how far performance criteria and standards are being achieved, and quality of service delivery attained.

By definition, indicators are 'surrogate' measures, that is, they usually represent a number of factors which might normally be difficult to evaluate. The indicators are usually selected on the basis that they will yield a reliable and valid assessment of performance.
c/f Performance criteria/Quality indicators/standards

Performance Standards

c/f Performance criteria/Standards

Permissive Legislation

This describes legislation which allows local authorities to provide services, but does not impose the duty upon them. Such legislation also empowers local authorities to delegate responsibilities to voluntary organisations providing welfare services. Some mandatory legislation ends up, because of the level of discretion allowed, virtually the same as permissive legislation.
c/f Discretion/Mandatory legislation

Personal Constructs

George Kelly originated the concept and use of personal constructs in psychology. They are used by social welfare staff in a number of settings including work with offenders, counselling, work with disruptive young people and drug users. Exercises can be created which encourage individuals to examine experiences and situations which they have found fun or painful; positive or negative; useful or of little value. By analysing these experiences, an individual, usually with help from a supervisor, can work out their own personal construct, or, put simply pre-disposition to types of experience. It is particularly helpful in analysing what motivates and de-motivates learners.
c/f Psychology

Personal Information

is an increasingly complicated and controversial area, as more
and more access is allowed to client or patient files and records.
Confidentiality rights can conflict with the moves towards open user
access, making the social welfare tasks of providing background
information for courts and assessing and monitoring behaviour
and needs a veritable balancing act. The Data Protection Act 1984
makes the keeping of computer and other data subject to registration
and inspection and other case law has informed social work and
probation practice with respect to complex areas such as child
protection, contraception, AIDs and HIV testing and criminal records.
In court proceedings, there is considerable pressure to make reports
more straightforward. The DHSS *Guidelines for Report Writing*
state: "Technical language not normally used by readers should
be avoided" and "overlong sentences with several sub-clauses".
The readers potential cited in the guidelines will include many lay
people – magistrates, parents and children.
*c/f Confidentiality/Pre-sentence reports/Recording/Social inquiry
report*

Personal Social Services

are the network of health care, community care, child care, probation
service and welfare benefits managed by the Secretary of State for
Social Services and administered by the Department of Health, Home
Office and the Department of Social Security. Many services are
provided in partnership with local voluntary organisations.
*c/f Benefits/Health Education/Probation and after-care service/Social
Work*

Pindown

The name of Pindown has become synonymous with an approach to
the treatment of young people with behavioural difficulties used in a
Staffordshire care facility. The Pindown regime used the restriction
of liberty and movement until young people would co-operate with
staff. The failure of the system and the ensuing public outcry led
to a re-assessment of work with severely disturbed and potentially
disruptive children in residential settings.

Pindown

The report about the specific Pindown affair written by Allan Levy QC and Barbara Kahan, and called *The Pindown Experience and the Protection of Children*, focussed especially on the restriction of liberty. The subsequent Children Act Guidance and Regulations (vol 4) published in 1991 lay down that secure accommodation and the restriction of children's liberty may only occur when a) a child has a history of absconding, *and* b) is likely to abscond from any other type of accommodation, *and* c) if the child absconds and is likely to suffer significant harm, *or* d) if kept in other types of accommodation, is likely to injure self or other people. However, many feel that the regulations are still too vague, and new guidelines are expected very soon.
c/f Children's homes/Community homes/Residential care/Secure accommodation

Play

is usually defined as behaviour freely chosen, self-motivated and involving fun. Play is thought to be a major source of educational stimulation and creativity for children. Many welfare workers are involved in directly providing or supporting the provision of facilities where children play, whether it is a mums and toddlers group in a community centre or a structured playcare facility aimed at offering care, supervision and educational opportunities. Play is believed to aid physical, emotional and intellectual development at different stages of a child's development. Playing with *things* is followed by playing with people, and then playing with ideas.
c/f Creche/Nursery/Playcare

Playcare

is a relatively new term which has been developed to describe play facilities which offer play within a care setting. Playcare is increasingly offered because children are seen as needing the same level of supervision from adults in play settings as they should receive in schools and the home. Playcare implies a contractual obligation between playcarers and parents, whereby the carers operate in loco parentis. By contrast, in open access play provision

Playcare (cont'd)

such as a cinema or swimming pool, children are free to come and
go as they please. The Children Act 1989 extended the duties of the
social services department to include regulation and registration of
play and care for children aged between five and seven.
c/f Latchkey children/Out-of-school clubs/Play/Playworker

Playgroups

are organised for children under five years of age. Staff do not
necessarily hold qualifications, but the group itself must be registered
with the local social services department.
c/f Nurseries/Play/Playcare

Playworker

Many staff working in a number of organisational settings with
younger children (roughly defined as pre-secondary school) are
known as playworkers. The places they work in are variously
called playgroups, playcare, adventure playgrounds, playschools,
playschemes, playbuses. The background of staff varies as does
the location of 'play' in the local authority structure. Leisure and
Recreation, Education, Social Services, Youth and Community
and Community Education are all potential managers and funders
of playwork, as are a wider range of voluntary organisations.
Playworkers' backgrounds can include teacher training, social work,
or sports and outdoor pursuits, arts and crafts qualifications, or
simply a keenness to work with children.
c/f Play/Playcare

Pluralism/Pluralist

This is a sociological term to describe a society where a number
of different communities of people, with diverse cultural, racial,
behavioural and religious beliefs co-exist. Pluralism is used to
describe a multi-racial society where the individual groups can
inter-act without overt aggression occurring.

   Pluralism in social welfare refers to the development of a mixture
of State, private and voluntary provision, which are resourced and
organised (in theory) to provide competition and choice. The Welfare

Pluralism/Pluralist

State is said to have become increasingly pluralist as a result of Conservative policies, which made much more extensive use of private sector services in health and social welfare.

Points System

In housing authority areas, the allocation of accommodation is based on a points system. Letting policy should be based on facts, and home visits are made to applicants to assess the applicant's current accommodation and special needs. Points are allocated based on current amenities (or rather lack of them), medical needs, disabilities, special circumstances (such as single parent, high priority, employment, homeless), length of time on waiting list. The points system is one part of the lettings process, but critics argue that it is still open to discretion and may lead to forms of discrimination.

Police

The police work closely with social welfare staff in a number of areas, in particular in court work, probation and child protection. The Police Act 1964 and the Police and Criminal Evidence Act 1984 are the main pieces of current legislation relevant to the organisation and structure, which is based on central and local government funding and local accountability.

The police force is charged with the responsibility of crime prevention, protecting members of the public and apprehending criminals. The political parties and the police themselves are in favour of more localised police organisation with more local accountability and multi-agency working in work with ex-offenders, disaster work and child protection. The police service in England and Wales is the responsibility of the Home Secretary.

Poverty

Poverty is normally accepted as lacking the means to subsist, usually defined in terms of money, accommodation, food, clothing and transport. There is no absolute definition, since levels of subsistence, the so-called *poverty line*, depend on government and society

Poverty (cont'd)

definitions of minimum standards. Social welfare responses through social work and health provision, benefits, universally available services and means-tested services are part of the response to poverty. Debate continues to surround the definitions for *absolute* and *relative*, and whether intervention or more radical social change is required to address the problem.
c/f Poverty trap/Social exclusion

Poverty Trap

Individuals and families are said to be caught in the poverty trap when they lose the power to increase their net earnings. This can happen when taxes are increased, but the most common cause of the problem is steeply tapered, means tested benefits, such as Housing Benefit. Increased earnings under the means tested system can actually make the recipient worse off as benefits are reduced by greater amounts than the increase in income. The effect of the poverty trap is to act as a disincentive to those seeking extra earnings, and many are forced to work in the black economy, receiving cash for menial forms of employment.
c/f Housing benefit

Pre-sentence Reports (PSRs)

are required when any court is considering a custodial sentence, probation order, community service order or supervision order. The Criminal Justice Act 1991 renamed the Social Inquiry Report as the Pre-sentence Report and changed its structure, particularly in respect of including a section on the seriousness of the offence and the offender's later view of their activity. The PSR also offers the social worker or probation officer's comments on the current offence; previous offending; risk to the public; and other background information and recommendations.
c/f Social inquiry reports

Presenting Problem

This is a 'jargon' term used by social workers to describe either the reason given by a client for requesting social work assistance, *or*

Presenting Problem

the official 'problem' which has been recognised by the agency.
The 'problem' may however not be the real cause of the difficulties
the client is experiencing or the behaviour which is being seen as a
problem needing help. Similar patterns exist for general practitioners
and social welfare staff who frequently need to look beyond the
superficial problem and try to identify a more fundamental malaise.
In work with offenders, probation officers and social welfare staff
are expected to look at the *whole* life of an offender rather than
concentrating on the offence alone, which was the presenting
problem.

Primary Health Care Team (PHCT)

The PHCTs provide the co-ordination for community health services.
Usually, they include members from a variety of professional
disciplines. They are frequently characterised as having loose
management structures and few common policies. Fund holding by
General Practitioners may lead to more integration of teams and
more formal team organisation.

Priority Estates Project (PEP)

was originally established by the Department of the Environment
in 1979. It has worked with over twenty local authorities on about
forty run-down and unpopular estates. The aim of PEPs is to
provide models of good local management practice involving direct
community and tenant participation.
c/f Estate action/Housing action trusts/Social housing

Prior Learning

c/f Accreditation of prior learning

Prison Service

The Prison Service provides the management and staffing in the
majority of prisons in the United Kingdom. In England and Wales, the
Home Secretary is responsible for the Prison Service and in Scotland
it is the Secretary of State for Scotland. Within the Home Office, the
Director General of Prisons is the senior official who works closely

Prison Service (cont'd)

with governors of individual prisons and the Home Office
Inspectorate of prisons. Prisons are supervised by Visiting
Committees and Boards of Visitors, which deal with disciplinary
matters. The Governor, together with various grades of prison
officers organises the individual prison regime, which will normally
include a mixture of work, training and education, and recreation.
Each prison also employs a range of social workers and medical staff
who assist the prison officers in the welfare of detainees.
c/f Prisons

Prisoners

People held in prisons and other penal institutions such as young
offenders' institutions are called prisoners or detainees. Although
prisons are designed to offer rehabilitation and training, research
has shown that most of the positive effects appear to be largely
outweighed by the negative effects of institutionalisation. Association
with other prisoners and alienation produce *criminalisation*, which
turns many offenders into career criminals, more likely to re-offend
than become reformed.
c/f Criminology/Detainees/Prisons

Prisons

together with some special hospitals provide the institutions where
offenders receive custodial sentences or punishment. The regimes
of different prisons vary considerably. The systems of *hard labour*
and *corporal punishment* have been abandoned, but liberty is still
curtailed, and solitary confinement as a further punishment, or for
the protection of prisoners likely to be victimised, continues to be
used. Prisons are supposed to 'encourage and assist prisoners to
lead a good and useful life', but as the number of violent prisoners
has risen, the pressure on the prison service has produced conflicts
between prisoners, prison officers and the prison governors. Prisons
are classified as *closed* or *open* and the prisoners requiring the
greatest level of security are committed to non-local, closed prisons.
The amount of training and rehabilitation work again varies between
prisons, but open prisons offer a more relaxed atmosphere and more
opportunity for training and study.

Prisons

Prisoner allocation for the more serious categories of prisoner is made by the Home Office. Local prison review boards handle other allocations. The Home Secretary and the Secretary of State for Scotland are responsible for all prison institutions in England and Wales, and Scotland, respectively. Prisons are individually managed by a Governor, and supervised by visiting committees and Board of Visitors. There are approximately 130 prisons, housing about 50,000 prisoners – but already private prisons are being contracted to take state prisoners.

c/f After care/Prison service/Probation/Punishment/Remand

Proactive

is a 'buzz-word' used in social work to describe approaches made by staff to actively change situations, influence people's attitudes and exercise leadership. Proactive approaches encourage staff to be more forward looking in their planning and actions, instead of purely reacting to crises and immediate problems. In community work, for example, benefits workers who actively encourage claimants to obtain their entitlements are working proactively, as are housing workers who encourage active tenant participation. Generally speaking, the term implies more strategic and preventative approaches to addressing social problems.

c/f Interactive/Reactive

Probation and After-care Service

The local administration of the probation and after-care service is organised through 55 area probation committees. Membership of these committees is made up of magistrates, judges, co-opted members and officials from the local authority probation service. These committees are responsible to the Home Office for the efficient functioning of the probation service, and are gradually being subject to more central control.

The aims and objectives of the probation service are the subject of considerable debate in the 1990s with the planned introduction of national standards for probation practice. The 1990 Green Paper *Supervision and Punishment in the Community* adds pressure

Probation and After-care Service (cont'd)

to make probation 'a criminal justice agency', but was first and foremost set up to respond to the wishes of the court.

Many probation staff, trained alongside social workers and used to assisting offenders and ex-offenders through pre-sentence reports, after-care work, community service supervision and conciliation work, are resistant to the move to make probation a service geared to directly confront offending through 'intensive' probation, which is as yet undefined.

c/f After-care/Licensees

Probation Order

This order is a sentence for offenders aged sixteen and over and requires the probation service to supervise the offender for a period of between six months and three years.

c/f Probation/Sentencing

Probation Reports

c/f Pre-sentence reports/Social inquiry reports/Welfare reports

Process Recording

is a specific type of recording or written record. The aim is to recreate everything that happened in a particular interview or event, including how the participants reacted to each other, what they did, and how they appear to feel. This record is of assistance in reflecting on 'what happened' in particular exchanges, and for supervision meetings, what might be done to improve practice skills.

c/f Recording

Professional Associations

A number of professional associations exist across the broad spectrum of social welfare. These aim to promote professional standards and improve the working conditions of their members. The British Association of Social Workers (BASW); National Association of Local Government Officers (NALGO); National Association of Probation Officers (NAPO); Social Care Association (SCA); British Association of Counselling (BAC); Health Visitors Association (HVA);

Professional Associations

Institute of Housing (IoH); Institute of Health Services Management (IHSM); National Association of Social Workers in Education (NASWE) and National Association of Youth and Community Education Officers (NAYCEO) are among the main ones.

Professional Development

is increasingly used to describe a wide variety of learning activities which take place to aid the professional development of an individual. The aim is to improve the knowledge, skill and expertise of a staff member. Training, supervision, support, assessment, appraisal and setting of personal development plans are all means of professional development.

Profiling

The activity of profiling, producing profiles and re-profiling is a technique for producing a statement about the characteristics of a service or organisation. When the service is re-organised or the needs of a client are re-assessed, their service needs are re-profiled to take account of those needs and existing service provision, and to highlight discrepancies between needs and priorities.
c/f Evaluation/Mapping

Prohibited Steps Orders

These court orders, under the 1989 Children Act, Section 8, are expected to be made rarely. They act as a means of preventing a parent taking particular steps without consent of the court. For instance, if a parent wished to change their child's school or withhold medical attention, the court might wish to over-rule them.
c/f Contact Orders/Divorce

Proportionality

is used in more than one context. In the justice system, it is used to describe the apportionment of justice, or making the punishment fit the crime. Social welfare staff involved in working with courts may find themselves swayed by both sides of the justice argument, for and against proportionality. Those in favour, stress the inherent fairness of a system which treats all offenders as being equal and

Proportionality (cont'd)

receiving a punishment related to the seriousness of the offence. Opponents favour a welfare approach which treats individuals as needing more personalised assessment and treatment.

In housing circles it is used to describe the relationship which is supposed to exist between local authority rents for council tenants, and tenants in assured tenancies in housing association and private sector accommodation.

c/f Justice/Sentencing/Social housing/Tariff system

Psychology

Psychologists study human behaviour and use their evaluation to suggest treatment plans. Psychology is the science of mind and behaviour and is the academic and practical discipline studied by students training to become educational or clinical psychologists. In social welfare, psychology is one of the underpinning theoretical disciplines used to make sense of the individual and societal problems which welfare workers try to solve or alleviate. Qualified psychologists are often part of the multi-disciplinary or multi-agency team working in mental health and child protection.

Psychometric Tests

are a range of tests used for assessing and predicting behaviour, attitudes and aptitude. There are many different test formats and their use must relate to the literacy, numeracy and cognitive ability of the person(s) to be tested. Many such tests require a professional psychologist to use them.

c/f Assessment/Rating scales

Psychosocial

is both a method of assessment and therapy, and a theoretical school or approach to social work intervention. The theoretical concepts of psychosocial development are based particularly on the work of Erik Erikson. The theory holds that every individual will experience predictable crises, phases of life and challenges. Psychosocial assessment and therapy concentrate on a mixture of

Psychosocial

psychological testing and an evaluation of environmental and inter-
personal influences. Intervention is then organised to help the client
overcome indentified problems and successfully function in society.

Psychosocial approaches tend to stress a flexible approach
to diagnosis and intervention, which takes account of changing
influences and circumstances.
c/f Assessment/Therapy

Psychotherapy

is a specialised form of therapeutic relationship usually established
to work with people suffering from mental health, relationship
and stress-related problems. The professional background for
psychotherapists often combines aspects of clinical psychology,
psychiatry and social work. A large number of psychotherapy
specialisms exist, including transactional analysis, psychoanalysis,
gestalt therapy and psychodrama.
c/f Transactional analysis

Punishment

is usually seen as having five (at least) purposes, and at times these
may conflict. The five purposes are: *retribution; protection and
prevention; reform, rehabilitation and education; deterrence;* and
reparation or *atonement*.

Punishment can be meted out through custodial, semi-custodial
(some restriction of freedom) or other forms such as fines, probation
orders and driving disqualification.
c/f Prison/Probation/Reparation

Purchaser – Provider Divide

Increasingly in the public sector, departments have established
separate *Purchaser Authorities* which are differentiated from the staff
employment (Provider) units. This has opened up market competition
and has led to public sector, private and voluntary organisations
competing for contracts. Perhaps the most developed examples exist
in the health service, where General Practitioners now purchase

Purchaser – Provider Divide (cont'd)

consultancy, diagnostic and acute hospital services, thereby creating the commonly called purchaser-provider divide.

Many local authority social services departments have reorganised their purchasing and providing divisions in order to discharge their responsibilities under the 1990 NHS and Community Care Act.

c/f Compulsory competitive tendering/Contracting out

Q

Qualitative Evaluation

complements statistical, quantitative analytic methods. Qualitative analysis/evaluation focuses on responses to programmes; aims and goals; skill transfer; ability, attitude and behaviour. In Community Arts, for instance, the evaluation of the artistry of a performance requires qualitative as well as quantitative evaluations.
c/f Assessment/Evaluation/Monitoring/Quality Indicators/Quantitative evaluation

Quality Assurance (QA)

developed from earlier methods of quality control. The International Standards Organisation in ISO 9000 defines Quality Assurance as: 'All those planned and systematic actions necessary to provide adequate confidence that a product or service will satisfy given requirements in quality.'

In social welfare, QA relates to all aspects of ensuring quality of service delivery, including recruitment and training and assessment through performance standards, audits and value analysis. To be effective, QA must have the full support of all involved and be 'owned' by staff.
c/f Audits/British Standard 5750/Quality circles/Standards/Total quality management/Value analysis

Quality Circles

are structured groups, usually of staff members and sometimes of service users, who meet together to discuss work-related problems and try to agree on solutions and strategies. The adoption of quality circles in social welfare has largely penetrated through from practice in the Health Service and from some management team-building initiatives. Circles work well if they have power to take action and if there is top management level approval of their functioning. They fail if there is distrust, no access to decision-making, and no

Quality Circles (cont'd)

understanding of wider quality assurance, TQM and 'ownership' questions.
c/f Quality assurance/Total quality management

Quality Indicators

These are outcomes which have been agreed as desirable for any organisation. Each indicator requires monitoring in order to assess how far the outcome is being achieved and what changes in service input may be required to improve the standard of service provided (outcomes). In social welfare, the majority of outcomes will be user-orientated. The indicators are used, for example, to measure the degree of customer satisfaction with services for older people in residential homes, or to monitor the effectiveness of social work *gate-keeping* in preventing inappropriate involvement of young people in the criminal justice system.

Performance indicators can be established to assess how far the service delivery is meeting the outcomes identified as quality indicators.
c/f Performance indicators/Quality assurance/Standards

Quantitative Evaluation

The growing use of performance indicators and performance standards, and other monitoring devices require a range of quantitative techniques. Tests and measurements which, for example, record numbers of users, outcomes, costs and any measurable variables are used in quantitative evaluation.
c/f Assessment/Evaluation/Monitoring/Qualitative evaluation

Questionnaire

A questionnaire is frequently used by social welfare staff to collect data about consumers, services and opinions of users and providers on the effectiveness of service delivery. Most questionnaires are presented in written form, but they can also be used by an interviewer or recorded on a computer programme.

The structure of questionnaires can be simple or complex and how the questions are organised is often described as being

Questionnaire

either *structured* or *unstructured* depending upon how flexible the framework is. A question which asks for a YES/NO tick box response is both structured and *closed*, relative to a question which has an *open* format and allows for any type or length of response.
c/f Assessment/Evaluation/Interactive/Monitoring

Quorate

c/f Quorum

Quorum

Some meetings in social welfare follow the rules of an organisation's standing orders, which determine the minimum attendance level for that meeting to take place. This minimum number is the quorum. In certain fields of welfare work, notably community work and community education, staff require a thorough understanding of the rules of meetings. For a meeting to be *quorate*, the quorum number must be achieved, otherwise it cannot take place and is deemed *inquorate*.
c/f Meetings

R

Racism

Racism implies negative action and attitudes used against a person or a group, based on stereotyping and unfair generalisation. Racism is a form of discrimination, and social work should be based on anti-discriminatory principles. Ensuring this in practice is more difficult.
c/f Discrimination/Equal opportunities/Ethnic minority

Random Sampling

is a type of research sampling technique used to understand the functioning of a particular group. A random sampling of young people looked after in care would be chosen without attempting to construct that sample on any representative criteria.
c/f Sampling

Rapporteur

In training workshops and seminars, rapporteurs are often appointed to take notes of key points arising from group discussion. They may then report back to any larger group meeting, or offer a written account of a conference or event.
c/f Workshops

Rating Scales

Rating scales, or rating tests are used to measure individual reactions to questions or statements usually in verbal or written questionnaires. The scales relate to the level of positive, neutral or negative response and can be used to assess attitudes.
c/f Attitudinal testing/Questionnaires

Reactive

describes actions taken in response to an immediate problem or crisis. It is also used to describe positively reacting to users' needs. High stress levels are created by a constant flood of situations

Reactive (cont'd)

demanding immediate responses, which in turn prevent more considered, or proactive approaches from being used. Where most intervention is organised as a reaction to pressure and demand, it will tend to create a vicious circle which is difficult to break into or change.
c/f Interactive/Proactive

Recidivism Rate

is the rate at which people return to institutions. In social welfare, recidivism rates are usually related to offenders (of different types) and to people who tend to lapse back into particular conditions or illnesses. Recidivism rates in mental hospitals, sex offenders and school refusal have all been relevant to the work of social welfare workers. For instance, in 1980, Rutter and Giller in *Juvenile Delinquency, Trends and Perspectives* (Penguin), found that in a large sample of East London boys, 68 per cent of adolescent delinquents had been regarded as 'troublesome' by their teachers at the age of eight.

Recidivist

A recidivist is someone who returns to a previous pattern of behaviour, or who returns to a particular type of institution. So, for instance, an offender who serves a second term in prison or a thief who habitually steals cars is a recidivist.

Reciprocity

is the balance between action and reaction. Within social welfare there are specific mutual agreements which are based on reciprocal action from the agencies and individuals involved. Local authorities and voluntary agencies are involved in a complex web of reciprocal services, and individuals in their role as citizens expect levels of service, but also have responsibilities. Informal care networks, good neighbour schemes, befriending and the like all work on the principle of reciprocity.
c/f Citizenship

Recognisance

This is a sum of money up to £1,000 which a parent or guardian is bound to pay if a juvenile commits a further offence after the court has agreed with the parent that they must exercise proper care and control. A recognisance can last for up to three years, but not beyond a juvenile's eighteenth birthday.
c/f Bound over/Breach proceedings/Sentencing

Recording

The activity of recording includes a range of techniques for keeping an account of what occurs in contact sessions between social welfare staff and their clients. In many instances, forms are constructed to make recordings systematic, making a record of an individual or group interaction comparable with any other. Recording, when made in a non-judgemental and unbiased manner, aids the process of providing support and assistance for clients and can help in assessment procedures. Written records are much used in social welfare work to aid assessments and inform decisions on intervention and support or treatment plans.

Problematic issues for workers and managers alike, are dealing with confidentiality, the question of access to personal information, the implications of the Data Protection Act, and the potential for biased and unfair recording.
c/f Assessment

Referral

is the rather pejorative and impersonal term to describe both the process where a person is directed towards a particular social welfare agency, service or resource, and the individual(s) concerned. An individual who chooses to use particular services or ask for help such as in the case of mental illness, is known as a self-referral. Because *labelling* can occur, the treatment of individuals as *referrals*, *cases* and *disposals* can actually reinforce their negative image. To make a referral, social welfare staff require sound knowledge of resources, alternative agencies, and need to have the ability to assess the needs of the client.
c/f Disposal/Labelling

Refugees

Social workers and health staff have become increasingly involved with refugees, particularly at times of war and famine. Refugees have been admitted into the United Kingdom, with or without full refugee status under the 1951 Convention relating to the status of refugees and the 1967 Protocol. Although social services departments and voluntary agencies are reluctant to encourage the movement of people from their own country to temporary residence in the UK, on occasions, as with the crisis in Bosnia, they have become involved in the care and support of the victims of the conflict. Voluntary organisations that specialise in refugee work include: Save the Children, the Ockenden Venture and Pestalozzi.

Refuges

are usually temporary *safe-places* for women or children who are at risk of abuse. Section 51 of the Children Act provides for the establishment of refuges for children in registered children's homes, voluntary homes or with an approved foster parent. Such refuges require a certificate from the Secretary of State. The Women's Aid Federation co-ordinates a network of safe, temporary accommodation for women and their children who have suffered physical or mental violence of any kind. The Children's Society have *safe houses* for runaway children, including those who have run away from children's homes.
c/f Children Act/Women's Aid

Registration and Inspection

Following the 1984 Registered Homes Act and subsequent legislation, nearly all residential establishments offering care and support for children, elderly people, people with physical disabilities, mental illness and learning difficulties are subject to registration and inspection by the local authorities. The regulation and inspection of day care services for the frail and the vulnerable is not yet in place, but seems set to be introduced. Similarly, the implementation of quality assurance, performance standards and competences of work will require an extension of the inspectorate role.

It has been suggested that the contracting-out of an increasing number of welfare services will leave the statutory departments with

Registration and Inspection

a residual role of registration, inspection and dealing with the client groups not contracted-out to voluntary and commercial services.
c/f Quality assurance/Residential care

Rehabilitation Advisors

This is the less common title for staff working in occupational therapy, normally with people with disabilities.
c/f Vocational rehabilitation

Relate

Formerly known as the Marriage Guidance Council, RELATE co-ordinates the selection and training of local counsellors for about 150 local marriage guidance councils. The training of counsellors is a major part of RELATE's work, since the range and complexity of relationship problems which may be presented by individuals and couples seeking advice is immense. Advice and counselling on marriage preparation and raising children is also available.
c/f Conciliation

Relaxation

is one of a wide range of therapeutic techniques sometimes used to help reduce stress. Relaxation methods are used in many group work situations. Control of breathing, tensing and relaxing of muscles; use of quiet, or music, and concentrated imagination are all ways of helping people to relax.
c/f Counselling/Groupwork/Therapy

Remand

Prisoners awaiting trial are on remand. Prison overcrowding is made worse by the numbers awaiting trial. The length of time on remand reached unacceptable levels in the 1980s, when some prisoners were held awaiting trial for over a year.
c/f Prison service/Prisons

Remission

is the reduction of a prisoner's sentence in return for that prisoner's good conduct. All prisoners except those serving a life sentence are eligible (as long as they have been sentenced to more than one month). Remission usually enables prisoners to gain release after serving only two thirds of the sentence. Prisoners serving life imprisonment may be released on licence from the Home Secretary, but are subject to recall to prison for the rest of their lives.
c/f Prisons

Rent Arrears

are the amounts of money owing to a landlord, whether local authority, housing association, co-operative, private person or commercial letting agency. Procedures are then put into effect in order to reduce and ultimately eliminate the arrears. If these fail, eviction usually results, following a Court Order.

Reparation

is a relatively new concept in social work with offenders. Reparation takes place usually under the supervision of a probation officer or social worker. An offender meets with the victim and agrees to payments to the victim or to undertake tasks and jobs as a means of making good or reparation. Reparation is also seen as offering the offender an opportunity to deal with their own sense of guilt.
c/f After-care/Compensation/Mediation/Probation

Reporter

The Reporter is the person to whom children are referred in Scotland if they are thought to be in need of compulsory measures of care. The Reporter makes initial investigations in the case and in approximately 50 per cent of cases does not recommend the calling of a Children's Hearing, (as established under the Social Work (Scotland) Act 1969). At a Children's Hearing, the Reporter acts as a legal adviser and recorder of decisions.
c/f Children's Hearings/Children's Panel

Research

is the term used for any systematic methods used to establish facts, principles or study behaviour, systems and outcomes. In social welfare settings many different kinds of research are undertaken: empirical studies usually conducted by academics; action research, operational research and programme evaluation are all forms of 'applied', as distinct from academic research.
c/f Assessment/Evaluation/Monitoring

Resettlement Units

Since 1985, the Secretary of State has been steering the Department of Social Security towards replacing resettlement units for single men (and some women). Twenty large scale resettlement units remain, offering institutional accommodation, medical advice and accommodation advice. Alternative, less institutional units run by voluntary agencies with DSS funding are expected to gradually replace the existing units.
c/f Homeless

Residence Order

Based on the principle that marriage may end, but parenthood does not, the Residence Order, under Section 8 of the Children Act 1989, means 'an order setting the arrangements to be made as to the person with whom a child is to live'. Such orders are increasingly flexible and can include directions dividing residence of a child between two parents.
c/f Contact Order/Divorce

Residential Allowance

Elderly people moving into residential homes run either by local authorities, private or voluntary agencies, all have their financial means assessed. Subsequently, residents are expected to contribute towards their accommodation. Residential Allowance is a benefit payable to residents in private and voluntary homes, but residents in local authority homes are not eligible for the allowance. This has financially penalised local authority residential homes and has led to the closure and transfer of local authority homes in many areas.
c/f Residential care homes for elderly people

Residential Care

Care in social settings involving residence in facilities away from the normal family living unit is described as residential care. The form of care programme provided varies enormously and depends upon factors such as needs, available resources, (including personnel and skills), and whether the individual has voluntarily chosen to live in residential care. Over 100 different types of residential care can be identified. The range includes special residential 'homes' and institutions for children, older people, and people with mental health and other illnesses or impairments. *Community Care* implementation is based on the assumption that support and care in the community is nearly always preferable to residential care on a 24-hour-a-day basis.

Examples of residential care include therapeutic communities for drug abusers; community homes for children; residential care homes for elderly people and sheltered accommodation.
c/f Community Care/Dependency/Institutions

Residential Care Homes for Elderly People

The provision of residential care homes is subject to the Registered Homes Act 1984. An increasing proportion of residential care homes are provided by the independent and commercial sectors, with about 100,000 people living in private sector homes. The local authorities in England still provide over 1,500 homes housing about 55,000 residents, but this number is gradually declining though contracting-out of services.

The local authority social services departments are responsible for the registration and inspection of all private and voluntary care homes. Financial advantages offered to the private sector have led the local authority sector to concentrate resources into larger units, look for links with health authorities to provide nursing and medical support, and develop *Resource Centres* for elderly people, offering a range of services. Further to these developments, many local authorities are considering the transfer of homes to housing associations and trusts.

Residents can expect personalised care and support in residential care homes, but not full time specialist medical or nursing care.
c/f Contracting out/Nursing homes/Residential care/Resource centre/Sheltered housing

Residential Schools

Schools for under 50 pupils *not* approved by the Education Act 1981 must register under the Registered Homes Act 1984. Most work with pupils with specific disabilities or learning difficulties. Other schools of less than 50 pupils are registered as community homes. Larger units are not registered but are inspected by Her Majesty's Inspectors of Schools, or social services staff if there is concern about child care.

As an area of work, there is great need for close co-ordination and co-operation between social services and education departments and voluntary and private agencies.

c/f Community homes/Residential care

Resource Centre for Elderly People

Since local authorities have begun to transfer residential homes to trusts and housing associations, and the private and voluntary sector homes have continued to grow, local authorities are concentrating their capital and revenue in a smaller number of homes. These new style homes are often designated as resource centres and offer a neighbourhood support service – day care, intensive home support, support for carers, an emergency call service as well as residential beds. This trend towards resource centres as the hub of local services is likely to continue.

c/f Community based services/Residential care homes

Respite Care

covers the range of temporary and emergency accommodation which may be made available by local authorities and voluntary agencies to help people in difficulty. In many cases, respite care may provide a break or breather away from the source of problems. For instance, carers looking after severely ill people may need respite from their labours. Refuges offer a type of respite from problems such as child abuse and wife battering.

c/f Refuges/Residential care

Revenue Support Grant

The majority of local authority expenditure is financed from central government through the Revenue Support Grant. Financial viability

Revenue Support Grant (cont'd)

for services such as the personal social services and education rely on accurate assessment by the government through the use of a complex statistical analysis called Standard Spending Assessments (SAAs). Only 14 per cent of local government expenditure is met out of local taxes, the remainder being funded from central government.
c/f Standard spending assessments

Role-models

Role-models are provided by people, who by virtue of their age, gender, ethnic background, experience and opinions offer potential models for emulation. In groupwork and in work with consumers who may need to increase their self-confidence and esteem, having positive role-models may offer alternative options for behaviour. Staff teams in youth and community work, for instance, usually need to reflect a diversity of cultural and age ranges to provide the most positive setting for growth and development.

In another sense, social welfare staff are also expected to behave according to the values and standards set for the profession of social work.
c/f Co-working/Groupwork

Role-Plays

are a training technique involving participants in acting out different roles and recreating situations which can then be analysed in terms of what happened, why, and what can be learned from the different roles people play in real life situations. In social welfare work, they are used both with clients and in staff training.
c/f Simulations

Rootless

c/f Homeless

S

Safe Sex

Safe sex should perhaps be referred to as safer sex. The idea is to promote contraception to prevent unwanted pregnancy and also help to reduce the spread of sexually transmitted diseases. Social work and health staff involved in health promotion programmes include advice giving and information on the range of contraceptives; condoms, the pill, diaphragm and coil.

c/f AIDS/Contraception/Health care/Health education/Sexually transmitted diseases

Safeguards/Safeguarding

Safeguards are sets of rules which form the basis for mutual agreement between clients or consumers and social workers, especially in groupwork. They can be embodied into a formal or informal contract, but are more usually agreed through discussion and group interaction. A typical set of safeguards would include agreement on confidentiality; attendance; participation and behaviour. Safeguarding as a process is often viewed as a means of empowering clients and helping participants to share ownership of a group.

c/f Boundary/Closed groups/Contracts/Groupwork

Sampling

takes place where a smaller group or subset of a total universe (or population) is used for research purposes to try and understand the functioning of the total group. A sample can be *randomly* chosen, or may be constructed or chosen as a *representative* sample of the whole population. For instance, sampling can be used to try and find out user responses to residential care services for elderly people, through interviewing a sample of the older people in a range of selected establishments.

c/f Quantitative evaluation

Schizophrenia

Patients diagnosed as schizophrenic make use of a considerable range of social welfare and health resources. The term tends to be used rather vaguely to cover a range of psychoses, where the individual suffers a change of personality; may feel controlled by alien forces and generally lacks motivation and emotional liveliness.
c/f Mental disorders/Mental ill health

Scottish Homes

was created as a government quango in 1989, to fulfil a similar function to the Housing Corporation in England, monitoring and funding housing associations. It succeeded the Scottish Special Housing Association and the Scottish Housing Corporation, and inherited housing stock, making it a direct housing provider, unlike its Welsh and English counterparts.
c/f Housing associations/Housing Corporation/Tai-Cymru

Section 2, Section 3, Section 4

Under *Section 2* of the Mental Health Act 1983, patients may be admitted for *assessment* because of a mental disorder. This disorder must warrant hospital admission because the patient is at personal risk or a danger to others. Application may be made by the closest relative or a social worker and two medical recommendations for compulsory hospital admission are required. Detention can last up to 28 days.

Section 3 applies to admissions to hospital where the mental disorder requires *medical treatment*. Patients may be kept for up to six months, which can be extended for a further six months, and thereafter by a year at a time.

Section 4 admissions under the same Act, apply to *emergency admissions* made on the recommendation of a single medical practitioner. The compulsory powers last up to 72 hours, but can be extended to 28 days if a second medical practitioner recommends extension.
c/f Mental disorders/Mental health

Section 29

is used as shorthand to describe vulnerable people, defined by
Section 29 of the National Assistance Act 1998. A local register
of people who are covered by the Chronically Sick and Disabled
Persons Act 1970 is required by statute to be kept by the local social
services department.
c/f Vulnerable people

Sectioning

is the loose term used for the procedure of admitting a person
suffering from a mental disorder into hospital for compulsory
assessment or treatment under the Mental Health Act 1983.
c/f Mental disorders/Section 2, Section 3, Section 4

Secure Accommodation

is defined as accommodation which restricts the liberty of a child
(Section 25, Children Act 1989). Only children who persistently
abscond or are regarded as a threat to themselves or others may
be held in secure accommodation. The same legislation states
that children can only be held in secure accommodation by a
local authority for up to 72 hours in any 28-day period. For any
longer period, a secure accommodation order granted by a court
is required. In *all* cases, a guardian ad litem is appointed to advise
the child. Secure accommodation may be used either for children
in care or under a supervision order, but it is only supposed to be
used as a *last resort*, especially since the Pindown enquiry. Secure
accommodation is governed by the Children (secure accommodation)
Regulations 1991. No child under thirteen may be placed in secure
accommodation without the prior approval of the Secretary of State.
c/f Children's homes/Community homes/Guardian ad litem/Pindown

Self-actualisation

is a concept originally associated with the work of psychologist,
Maslow. "Be all you can be" has been used by a number of health
and welfare organisations to promote the public's awareness of
their own potential and power to alter and change their lives. Social
welfare staff sometimes describe the process of enabling clients to

Self-actualisation (cont'd)

take on new ways of being, acting and thinking as self-actualisation. Used in this way, the term is equivalent to *consciousness-raising*, but pitched at a more individualised level, and with the explicit assumption that the person will act to bring about self-change.
c/f Consciousness-raising/Empowerment/Self-awareness/Self-help

Self-advocacy

is encouraged under initiatives such as Community Care. It describes a process where people speak for or represent themselves. In social care, staff can encourage self-advocacy through various forms of confidence-building and empowerment. It is particularly important in relation to vulnerable people, such as individuals with mental health problems.
c/f Advocacy/Empowerment/Vulnerable people

Self-awareness

Is also known as *self-knowledge*. Much social welfare work is based on a need for staff to understand their own beliefs, strengths and weaknesses, and to encourage a process of similar discovery by clients. Self-awareness is one step towards taking action which allows for change. Much counselling, interviewing and groupwork is based on techniques and exercises designed to improve an individual's capacity to risk change and understand how their actions affect others. The effectiveness of the process depends on the individual's capacity for critical reflection about themselves and their experiences.
c/f Assertiveness/Empowerment/Self-actualisation

Self-help

Self-help implies taking responsibility for one's own problems and doing something about them. Helping people to attain independence of statutory services in social welfare and health, is a primary aim of these services. This reflects a new phase of the Welfare State. Getting people to help themselves is part of the social welfare task, and self-help has come to be seen as both an individual and a collective activity. Particularly in the areas of disability, race and

Self-help

sex discrimination, illness and unemployment, groups of people have formed for mutual support and to promote awareness and understanding of their personal issues. Social welfare staff in both voluntary and statutory organisations have been active in stimulating self-help, within both right and left political ideologies.
c/f Self-actualisation/Self-awareness/Voluntary agencies

Sensory Impairments

This term is used to cover the range of impairments which deprive people of one or more of their senses. Deafness and blindness are the two most common, and increasingly people suffering with either condition are referred to as people with sensory deprivation.

Sentencing

is undertaken by judges and magistrates after hearing a criminal case in court. The sentences available to courts are also known as the *tariff system*. The principles of sentencing are based on a need to protect the public; deter offenders through punishment; rehabilitate and educate criminals and offer compensation and reparation to victims of crime.

The main range of sentencing options in criminal proceedings are: hospital or guardianship order; imprisonment; suspended sentence; curfew order; combination order (probation and community service order); community service order; attendance sentence order; probation order; supervision order; fine; compensation order; conditional discharge; absolute discharge.
c/f Courts/Proportionality/Tariff system

Serps

stands for the state earnings-related pension scheme which was first established in this form in 1978.

Services Strategy

involves planning ways in which services can best be provided to meet needs effectively. Usually it involves prioritisation and choice, and increasingly, consumer consultation and involvement. A service

Services Strategy (cont'd)

strategy might, for instance, involve always using fostering and adoption services, wherever possible, in preference to residential care.
c/f Strategic planning

Sexism

describes individual actions and attitudes and institutional or organisational systems which discriminate against and disadvantage people because of their gender. In social care, changes in equal opportunities legislation and training, awareness and assertiveness workshops and changes in attitudes and language, alongside management practice are ways of combating sexism.

Sexually Transmitted Diseases (STD)

The support and treatment of people with a range of sexually transmitted diseases is principally a health concern, but since information and advice may be requested from social welfare staff, most workers and organisations try to keep information of STDs and sources of help and advice available. Treatment of STDs is undertaken in strictest confidence and is free. Patients can self-refer without contact with their general practitioner. The range of STDs is considerable, including what are known as venereal diseases, acquired through sexual contact, such as gonorrhoea, syphilis, herpes and AIDs.
c/f AIDs/HIV

Sheltered Housing

This is a form of supported accommodation primarily developed for the care in the community of elderly people. Sheltered housing is a descendent of almshouse accommodation, and providers include housing associations, local authority housing departments and a few social services departments. Tenants are encouraged to live independently in self-contained living units with assistance from a usually resident warden. Such housing is frequently referred to as 'Category 1 & 2', category 1 being intended for younger, fitter tenants, (based on the Ministry of Housing circular 82/69, which is

Sheltered Housing

influential, but no longer mandatory upon the public sector). With an increasingly elderly population, more schemes are now classified as providing *extra* care; with communal facilities and a wider range of care support from a range of service providers.

Sibling Rivalry

means, simply, brothers and sisters who compete and do not get on very well!

Significant Harm

is the legal term used to describe the range of dangers faced by children who may be made subject to a care order under section 31 of the 1989 Children Act.
c/f Care Order/Child protection registers

Simulations

are complex exercises, often used in social welfare staff and client training. Simulations recreate situations as learning experiences, and can be co-operative, competitive, group or individually oriented. For instance, staff may engage in a simulation which looks at the way staff are interviewed for a particular post. This type of simulation would include role-playing an interview panel and the applicants for the post.
c/f Critical incident analysis/Role-plays

Social Care

This term is frequently used as a synonymous term with *social welfare*, and as an alternative to *social work*. It describes systems of intervention designed to help and support members of the community. It often implies wider professional and voluntary, formal and informal, networks of support and assistance which can include neighbours in local communities offering friendship and practical assistance, through to the services provided for special needs groups by social services, residential homes, general practitioners and hospitals.

Social care (cont'd)

The practice of social care is usually seen both as incorporating *social work*, and being a much wider process. Social care practitioners are those employed in community, domiciliary and residential care services, who provide direct, practical care, often in partnership with staff from other professions. The status of social care staff is generally seen as lower than social workers, because many are employed on manual grades, and perhaps because the vast majority are women. The Social Care Association is the main professional organisation working on behalf of staff employed in residential, day and domiciliary services as direct practitioners and managers.
Care/Community Care/Health care/National Vocational Qualifications/ Social work

Social Control

Interventions by social welfare workers are frequently forms of social control for their clients. Many work programmes with offenders and clients who have difficulties in dealing with aspects of their lives – drugs, drink, relationships, violence, and so on – encourage clients to learn or adopt new patterns of behaviour which enable them to reduce their level of threat to society as a whole.

In a wider sense, social control is the pressure exerted by people and organisations which establish patterns and forms of behaviour generally believed to be 'normal' or 'acceptable'. These social norms are frequently reinforced through laws and agencies working to enforce the laws, which are sometimes referred to as agents of social control.
c/f Agents of social control/Behaviour modification/Social norms

Social Education

is used to describe most forms of educational input which are focused on personal social learning. These include learning about relationships, rights and responsibilities and leisure and sports activities. Social Education forms the curriculum for many pastoral care teachers, youth workers and youth counsellors who are concerned with the problems young people (and sometimes older people) have in learning about, and coping with society.
c/f Pastoral care

Social Education Centres

Also previously known as Adult Education Centres, Social Education Centres are being established to help people with learning disabilities. Many courses based both inside and away from these centres are aimed at improving employment and social skills. Responsibility for such services for training and occupation lies with the local authority under the National Health Service Act 1977.

Many social education centres work with a mixture of physically disabled and mentally handicapped people and people with a range of learning disabilities.

c/f Learning disability/Special needs

Social Exclusion

Under the European Social Charter, social exclusion was the term used as a synonym for poverty, and those suffering from poverty were deemed as socially excluded.

c/f Poverty/Poverty trap

Social Fund

This fund was established in 1987–88, and is the general title for payments made by the Department of Social Security in cases of emergency. Most of the payments are discretionary and the fund is locally managed, meaning that it can run out. Non-discretionary funds are available through the Social Fund for funerals, maternities and in the case of cold weather. Specific Social Fund grants are available to people leaving residential care and as loans for crises.

Social Goals

are frequently the aims of social welfare interventions, which may be publicly stated in mission statements and policy documents. Some social goals are broad, like reducing crime, homelessness and poverty, whilst others are more specific, such as diverting people from custodial sentences. Social goals in welfare work can sometimes be contradictory, for instance, *empowerment* can be one goal, but *behaviour modification* and *socialisation* may also be used with some client groups!

c/f Socialisation/Welfare state

Social Housing

is the term most frequently used to describe what is commonly
referred to as *council housing*. Social housing most usually
means all housing which has been made available through public
expenditure, but can also be used to refer to housing owned through
housing associations and co-operatives. With the 'Right to Buy' the
Conservative government under Margaret Thatcher stimulated home-
ownership and by 1992, 1.4 million former council house tenants had
bought their homes.

In the 1990s, through large-scale voluntary transfer of stock, many
former local authority tenants now rent property administered by
housing associations.
c/f Housing associations/Voluntary transfer

Social Inquiry Reports (SIRs)

The preparation of reports to assist courts in considering the
most appropriate action in an individual case is the responsibility
of probation and social services staff. These reports follow a
standard structure covering home background, education, health
and any other relevant information. The Social Inquiry (or Enquiry)
Report is also made available to the individual concerned and their
representative. SIRs under different legal proceedings are prepared
simultaneously with any investigation regarding criminal behaviour.
The SIR is designed to make choosing a *disposal* more likely to
produce the maximum benefit. Social enquiries are also made in
matrimonial disputes. Conflict over whether the SIR is designed
to help the individual concerned, or only the court, continues to
exist in many cases. Under the 1991 Criminal Justice Act, social
inquiry reports prepared for presentation at courts are known as
pre-sentence reports.
c/f After-care/Disposal/Pre-sentence report/Probation/Social work

Social Landlord

is the name given to local authorities and the various forms of
housing associations who operate as landlords to tenants and
co-owners in social housing.
c/f Housing associations/Social housing

Social Norms

are established through laws and institutions in society. They are the acceptable forms and patterns of behaviour which are reinforced by rules and laws. Much social welfare work has a correctional nature, exerting influence to modify behaviour which is deviant from the morally and socially acceptable 'norm'. Child sexual abuse, truancy and homosexuality are all regarded by the law as being divergent from the social norms of current society, although within certain cultural sub-groups, their social-norm may include behaviour generally seen as unacceptable.
c/f Social control/Socialisation

Social Security

is the successor to the *Poor Law*, which in the nineteenth century provided state assistance only for those who could prove 'need'. Social Security is often defined as all the financial arrangements made by the State to alleviate poverty. For most of the twentieth century there have been three elements to social security: a) assistance given on the proof of need – means testing; b) national insurance, which covers many people when they are sick or of pensionable age, and c) universal allowances, such as child benefit.

Since 1979, the successive Conservative governments have taken a critical approach to what they have called the 'dependency culture'. Increasingly, benefits are becoming means-tested, and focused on special needs groups.
c/f Poverty trap

Social Services

After the Seebohm report, the 1970 Social Services Act was passed which effectively established the profession of the modern social services. The Act required local authorities to establish social services committees, under the national oversight of the Secretary of State in the Department of Health. The actual responsibilities and functions of the social services change through time, and are expressed in the detail of particular legislation such as the Children Act 1989, the Registered Homes Act 1984 and the NHS and Community Care Act 1990. Broadly speaking, the statutory social

Social Services (cont'd)

services departments exist to provide support for individuals and communities experiencing social and emotional difficulties. The specific services are not always requested by the clients, and so the current concern for partnership working between service providers and consumers, sits somewhat uncomfortably with the imposition of assessment, treatment and other forms of direct intervention. The social services are also seen as having a preventative role, designed to alleviate hardship and prevent suffering.

c/f Personal social services/Social work qualifications/Social worker

Social Skills

are the skills which enable individuals to communicate with, and interact with others in society. Many vulnerable users of social welfare services require support in developing their social skills. These skills, such as speaking effectively in public, writing intelligibly, and communicating at interviews, are often developed through social groupwork co-ordinated by social welfare staff. Specialist social skills required by many social work staff include empathy, counselling and listening skills.

c/f Groupwork

Social Welfare

is the umbrella term to cover the range of the benefits and services provided by the State and through voluntary activity to meet the social, educational, health and economic needs of the population.

c/f Social care/Social services/Social work

Social Work

is the *profession* which employs a range of social work staff in local authorities and, increasingly, voluntary agencies. These staff use a variety of methods, including casework, groupwork and community care which are aimed at enhancing the lives of individuals and family groups, assisting with problems and improving their social conditions. Counselling, advocacy, therapy and community organisation can all be part of the service provided by social work agencies. Many social work agencies stress the adoption of

Social Work

professional and ethical standards and the understanding of human development and behaviour as requisites for professional social work practice. Training for the profession of social work is organised through colleges and universities, and the Care Sector Consortium who are co-ordinating the National Vocational Qualifications. The Central Council for Education and Training in Social Work validate all professional courses of social work training. Local authority social services are managed in England, Wales and Scotland under the general guidance of the Secretary of State for Social Services, the Secretary of State for Wales and the Secretary of State for Scotland, respectively.

c/f Care management/Community care/Community social work/Social work qualifications/Social worker

Social Work Associates

is a relatively recent term which is being used to describe a range of staff who are not qualified social work staff, but who provide specific functions. The term has been more in vogue in the United States, where associates perform an ever increasing range of functions.

Social Work Qualifications

The Central Council for Education and Training in Social Work is responsible for validating professional social work training. By 1994–95, it is intended that there will only be one basic professional qualification, the Diploma in Social Work (Dip SW) which lasts a minimum of two years. Until then, the Certificate of Qualification in Social Work (CQSW) and the Certificate in Social Service (CSS) continue to be offered. Course content requires candidates to attain set standards of knowledge, skills, values and competence. A range of post qualifying studies are also promoted by CCETSW.

c/f Social work/Social worker

Social Worker

This is the generic term in local authorities and many voluntary organisations used to describe staff working with people who are experiencing problems, which may be personal, family-related,

Social Worker (cont'd)

practical, physical, mental or emotional. Some social workers assist the whole range of possible clients, whilst others are appointed to specialist posts dealing with particular client groups such as children or deaf people, or with specific tasks such as adoption and fostering. Qualifications for social workers are validated by CCETSW. In other related settings, social workers include: hospital social workers; psychiatric social workers; intermediate treatment officers; Education Welfare Officers and Housing Welfare Officers who are also considered as social work staff by many authorities.
c/f Generic/Social work/Social work qualifications/Specialist

Socialisation

is a process where individuals or groups of people learn, or are taught, the values and behaviours which are acceptable within a particular community or society. Failure to become 'socialised' frequently leads individuals into positions where society's agencies of control – police, courts, education, social work, and so on – decide that compensatory 'socialisation' is required. In welfare work, this may mean that an individual receives individual or group treatment or therapy with an aim to changing attitudes and producing acceptable patterns of behaviour.
c/f Behaviour modification/Labelling/Social control/Social norms

Sociogram

Sociograms are used in some social groupwork and training situations to offer a diagramatic or graphic representation of how a group and its members interact. Sociograms can be designed to record the frequency and type of contribution made by different members, and can also show alliances and antagonisms, form and change.
c/f Groupwork/Recording

Software

Software, in computing, is the name for all programs whether accessed from disk, or resident in a computer's hard disk drive. Software programs are increasingly bespoke, designed to monitor

Software

social welfare systems, and run office requirements through word processing spreadsheets and data management.
c/f Monitoring/Hardware

Special Educational Needs

The 1981 Education Act, which was implemented in 1983, introduced the concept of children with 'special educational needs'. Local education authorities have the responsibility for identifying all children with any sort of learning difficulties, and for making appropriate education available. This can include social work and other specialist involvement from professionals such as educational psychologists, speech therapists and physiotherapists. The 1981 Education Act also placed a duty on LEAs to provide education in ordinary schools rather than in special schools wherever possible.
c/f Special needs

Special Needs

Social welfare staff deal with a diverse range of needs, many of which are deemed 'special'. *Special needs* include needs which are special because of difficulties with learning, physical impairment, and emotional, social and intellectual development. In different contexts, such as housing and community work, special needs groups can also include: single parents, ethnic minorities and women. The term tends to be used loosely, and even when incorporated into legislation, special needs can be used to describe either a group of people or a condition which a group has in common.
c/f Special educational needs

Special Schools

These schools provide on-site and off-site education for children assessed as requiring special tutoring, treatment and support because of learning difficulties and disabilities. Such schools tend to have multi-disciplinary staff teams and may include staff with specialist training in social work, speech therapy, psychology, counselling and physiotherapy. Children assessed as having special

Special Schools (cont'd)

educational needs have a right to educational provision from the age of three until they reach their nineteenth birthday.
c/f Special educational needs/Special needs

Specialists

Many social welfare staff in the 1980s and 1990s have become more specialist both in terms of the skills they need to perform tasks competently, and in the client or consumer group with which they work. In practice teams, child protection work is one of the largest specialisms; whilst in management, quality assurance is a new and growing area of technical expertise.

Specific Issue Orders

are orders 'giving directions for the purpose of determining a specific question which has arisen, or which may arise in connection with any aspect of parental responsibility for a child'. Used by courts under the Children Act, 1989, Section 8, the aim is to prevent potential risks to a child, or settle parental disputes in such cases as school or church attendance.
c/f Contact orders/Divorce

Standard Spending Assessments (SSAs)

In local authority areas the government assesses the amount of money to which the authority is entitled under the Revenue Support Grant. The SSAs are calculated using a complex analysis of potential user numbers for services, and special factors such as social deprivation which produce statistical formulae for working out costs plus costs relating to geographical location (London and the South-east being more expensive). The areas of service covered in SSAs are: a) Education, b) personal social services, c) police, d) fire and civil defence, e) highway maintenance, f) all other services, g) capital financing.
c/f Revenue support grant

Standards

The term 'standards' has a variety of applications. In relation to the National Vocational Qualifications, standards are the measure

Standards

or level of performance or skill required to be adjudged competent relative to previously agreed performance criteria. Standards and standard-setting are used in Quality Management, and increasingly standards of performance are written and made explicit, dealing with the quality or performance indicators which allow for assessment and critical analysis. For instance, a service for people with learning disabilities can be assessed against the indicators: how many people with learning disabilities live in their own homes? What proportion are these of the whole? All people with learning disabilities will have an individual care plan based on an assessment of individual strengths and weaknesses.

There is an International Standard for quality assurance IS 9000 and British Standard BS 5750 (pt 2) which interpret the term for social care agencies. It is based mainly on applying good management practice to common-sense principles such as keeping records and verifying quality control.
c/f British Standard 5750/National Vocational Qualifications/ Performance criteria

Statutory Services

The statutory services are those which are provided by the government and local authorities as a direct responsibility laid down in legislation. In social welfare, the statutory authorities are principally in social services, health, education, probation, police, housing and employment services.

Confusingly, the statutory services often rely on the so-called voluntary services or agencies such as the NSPCC to carry out the provision and themselves perform the registration and inspection functions and act as purchasers rather than direct providers.
c/f Personal social services/Voluntary agency

Strategic Planning

is an important management tool to ensure that services are being effectively organised to define goals and identify methods of attaining them. Increasingly, multi-agency teams in health and social services are being established to make assessments of need, evaluate

Strategic Planning (cont'd)

priorities and allocate resources to achieve results. Strategic planning implies long or medium term planning and goal setting for the re-evaluation of current services and programmes.
c/f Services strategy

Structural Variables

This is an academic term to describe social and economic conditions; employment and unemployment; housing and educational opportunities. Structural variables are one of the major factors which can create, or contribute to individual problems. Social welfare interventions are sometimes aimed at making improvements to these variables.

Summarising

Counsellors and group-workers sometimes use 'summarising' as a tool to help clients on the most important aspects of problems. Summarising can take place at the beginning of a session or during a session and can help to organise discussion and thought processes. The technique of summarising also provides reassurance for the client and affirmation that they are valued and being listened to.
c/f Counselling/Focussing/Groupwork

Summative Evaluation

usually occurs near the end of the life of a project or welfare programme and is frequently concerned with *achievements* and *outcomes*. It gets its name from being a summation of the value and progress made by a particular agency or project.
c/f Formative evaluation

Supervision Order

'Supervision' in legal terms relates both to children *at risk* under the Children Act 1989, and *young offenders* under the Children and Young Persons Act 1969. This separation was an important aspect and intention of the 1989 legislation. A supervision order places a child or young person under the supervision of a local authority or probation officer. The conditions for children at risk and young

Supervision Order

offenders are agreed by the court and can include detail on: accommodation; specific attendance at places and times; involvement in particular programmes of activities; name of supervisor and 'responsible person' having parental responsibility for a child.

Children Act orders last initially for one year, whereas Children and Young Persons Act orders can be made for up to three years. The particular conditions attached to the order for criminal supervision make it possible for magistrates to punish and restrict control, making it an alternative to custody in the tariff system.

Care Order/Education Supervision Order/Family Assistance Order/Sentencing/Tariff system

Support

Social workers and other social welfare staff offer a vast array of general and specialist support to members of the community. The word 'support' is often used to describe the aim of social welfare services being to offer *support and assistance* to families, children, older people, offenders, victims, people suffering from disabilities and others with special needs.

Confusingly, and perhaps patronisingly, 'support' is also the term used to describe services made compulsorily, and sometimes against the wishes of the recipient.

c/f Care/Social care/Supervision/Supervision Order

Support and Care

In particular contexts, such as housing, the phrase 'support and care' is being substituted for special needs. Terms such as the provision of housing *with* support and care, and Support and Care Housing are becoming common.

c/f Special needs

Synergy

In social welfare management and training, synergy describes the process where group action and co-operation can be harnessed to produce more effective outcomes. The belief is that synergy is

Synergy (cont'd)

produced through active collaboration, thereby creating a result which is greater than the output of the individuals (or agencies) participating.

Systems Intervention

Social work systems should serve to assist consumers with their problems and empower them towards positive independence. Systems intervention is usually used to describe policies and procedures which determine how consumers in social welfare should be serviced, in order to most accurately assess and meet their needs. It is often used in the context of avoiding undue formal processing or inappropriate interventions from welfare staff.
c/f Diversion/Gate-keeping/Net-widening

Systems Theory

An approach for analysing phenomena and events as interrelated 'worlds' not just as their discrete parts.

Understanding the human social system and all the sub-systems is the pre-occupation of many researchers and social planners. Sociology, psychiatry and psychology have provided interesting insights into understanding how whole systems work and how different systems interact. In social welfare, systems theory has underpinned a number of models of social work practice, sometimes referred to as a unitary approach. Systems approaches have also encouraged social work managers to try to understand all the influences on individual clients, and to see the networks of services as a resource system, which can be mobilised to meet the assessed needs of individuals and communities.
c/f Systems intervention/Unitary model

T

Tai-Cymru

in Wales has the same function with regard to funding and monitoring the running of housing associations as the Housing Corporation does in England. Operated as a virtual government quango, it is controlled by a board appointed by the Secretary of State for Wales.
c/f Housing associations/Housing Corporation/Scottish Homes

Take-up

applies to the claiming of benefits and services. The take-up rate of benefits and services can be monitored, and welfare rights work is predominantly concerned with encouraging those eligible to take up their rights to services and benefits. Low take-up rates are often blamed on poor publicity, too much bureaucracy and form filling, social stigma and the complexity and changing structure of available services and benefits.
c/f Benefits/Social security/Welfare rights

Target System

is used to describe the *object* of social work intervention, which can be an individual, organisation or community. As a system, it allows staff to establish aims and measure effectiveness. For instance, to achieve less vandalism on a particular housing estate, social workers may have to work with all members of the community, the police and education staff to effect changes in attitudes towards, and facilities for, young people.
c/f Client system/System theory/Systems intervention

Tariff System

The tariff system is used specifically in social work and court-related circles to describe the sentencing policy based on the assertion (Home Office 1990 *Crime, Justice and Protecting the Public*) that "punishment in proportion to the seriousness of the crime . . . should be the principal focus of sentencing decisions".

Tariff System (cont'd)

Proponents of the tariff system argue that a justice model which establishes penalties and sentencing for different offences is fair and equitable. Some offenders will also argue the same line, since many regard court sentencing policy and practice as an unfair lottery. Others feel that justice without individual welfare runs contrary to a fair and caring society.

c/f Justice/Proportionality/Sentencing

Task-centred Casework

focusses on helping a client to identify problems and tasks which will help to resolve the problems. The casework relationship between the worker and the client is usually time-limited, and may be agreed in a contract. It was originally developed in America, largely as a means of 'professionalising' the relationship-building and problem-solving aspects of casework with social welfare clients.

c/f Casework/Contracts

Tenant Participation

A wide range of social welfare workers employed by local authority social services and housing departments and through voluntary agencies are expected to promote tenant participation. Tenant involvement in community decisions on housing has been a platform of Conservative government policy, but the idea of greater tenant participation is supported by all the major political parties and the national housing organisations. What exactly constitutes tenant participation is a matter which causes considerable debate. Involvement in management of housing and planning for changes in services; consultation and information-sharing; tenant choice in service providers and landlords are all cited as examples of tenant participation. Different local authorities, housing associations and housing co-operatives have tried a variety of methods, and processes to empower tenants, but tenants are often suspicious of tenants' consultations if they are not given the power to enact change and improve existing services.

Tenant Participation

A Tenant Participation Advisory Service (TPAS) exists in England and Scotland. Each operate as membership organisations providing information, training and advice on tenant involvement.
c/f Housing associations/Social housing

Tenant Participation Advisory Service (TPAS)

c/f Tenant participation

Tenant's Charter

The Tenant's Charter was established under the 1980 Housing Act. Tenants have security of tenure under the Charter, a right to repair, a right to sub-let, and a right to be consulted if the local authority is considering disposal of council house stock to a private landlord or housing association. The right to buy housing stock was also established under the 1980 Act, and had led to about 1.4 million former council tenants owning their homes by 1992. The Tenant's Charter has evolved through the 1990s (the 1985 Housing Act consolidated many of the charter rights) and seems set to continue to do so with a new 'Right to improve'.
c/f Citizenship/Housing associations/Social housing/Tenant's guarantee/Voluntary transfer

Tenant's Choice

c/f Voluntary transfer

Tenant's Guarantee

is the name given to the guarantees which apply to tenants in housing association accommodation. The Housing Acts of 1985 and 1988 established the Tenant's Guarantee which gives the Housing Corporation powers to ensure that all registered housing associations comply with the guidelines. These include making accommodation accessible to people on low incomes, whether or not they are in employment or in receipt of housing benefit and offering assured tenancy agreements. Managers of housing associations must ensure that the minimum standards of

Tenant's Guarantee (cont'd)

housing management practice are achieved as required under the
Guarantee.
*c/f Affordability/Housing associations/Housing Corporation/Tenant's
Charter/Voluntary transfer*

Terminally Ill

Care for terminally ill people can take place in a variety of community
and residential settings and will frequently involve social care staff.
The aim of such care is to make the person as comfortable as
possible, but control of pain and a sympathetic face and ear are also
important. Often non-professionals find it easier to show emotion
and offer real care and empathy for the dying. Professional staff can
frequently find this work uncomfortable and may avoid contact with
the terminally ill person.
c/f Bereavement/Hospices

T-Group

This is a formal, structured training group, usually consisting of
staff who regularly work together. The style of T-groups is meant
to further co-operative approaches to problem-solving, better
communication and self-awareness.
c/f Groupwork

Therapy

is the generic term for any of a number of systematic treatment
programmes aimed at reducing or curing the individual effects of a
physical or mental condition or problem. For instance, some social
welfare staff co-ordinate therapeutic programmes for substance
abusers, victims of child abuse, and their abusers. Therapy
should involve a planned programme of activity, counselling and
group meetings, designed to resolve individual problems. Where
therapy involves residential living, those involved are often called
a *therapeutic community*. In practice, therapy usually implies a
measure of self-help as well as outside intervention.
c/f Counselling/Groupwork/Treatment

Third Age

This is a relatively new term used to describe the period of life beyond middle age. Its proponents stress the Third Age as a positive period, where knowledge of life and experience provide the basis for making a continued and positive contribution to society. This is set against a natural decline in some physical and mental powers evident in the ageing process.
c/f Ageism/Older people

Three Es, The

The three Es were developed by the Audit Commission following on from the 1982 Finance Act, as the main purposes of a quality approach to ensure that resources are used: economically, efficiently and effectively.
c/f Audit/Quality assurance

Token Economy

is a therapeutic procedure using 'tokens', which are given to residents in some care settings when they successfully perform a particular activity. It is a form of behaviour modification, which reinforces positive behavioural patterns.
c/f Behaviour modification/Milieu therapy/Residential care

Tolerance

In addition to the common meaning of 'ability to endure', it is also used in the context of drug use or misuse, to describe a user's ability to function under regular use of a drug. The pattern of drug use usually means that it takes higher doses of a drug to maintain the same level of effectiveness, whether it is for medical or social purposes.
c/f Drug dependency/Drug use

Total Quality Management (TQM)

is a term usually used to describe a further development of Quality Assurance as a holistic, or corporate, application of the QA philosophy to every aspect of an organisation's system(s). It is consumer-focussed and stresses quality of service as the first

Total Quality Management (TQM) (cont'd)

essential of operation. The TQM culture is one of encouraging enthusiasm and ownership of services and meeting or exceeding the expectations of consumers. In social welfare work, there are some areas such as work with offenders, where it is hard to ask for consumer feed-back for a service they have been ordered to receive! But the concept of *best possible* service quality, linked to the *value for money* ethic of quality control has won many converts.
c/f British Standard 5750/Quality assurance

Training and Enterprise Councils (TECs)

The TECs were established through the Training and Education Directorate to co-ordinate, regionally, training and vocational education. The primary aim is to improve the skill level of the labour force through youth and adult training. The TECs are being encouraged to form partnerships with local education authorities to enhance the careers service and careers guidance. Employment Training and Youth Training are the responsibility of the TECs in England and Wales and the Local Enterprise companies in Scotland.
c/f Enterprise and Education Directorate/Training

Training, Enterprise and Education Directorate (TEED)

Since 1990, the Directorate has taken over all functions from the old Training Agency and Manpower Services Commission. This includes responsibility for training, enterprise and education policy; contract management for local training and enterprise councils (TEC's), local education authorities (LEAs), local enterprise agencies and other bodies; work on training standards and systems, and direct delivery of special programmes such as the Small Firms Local Guarantee. The Directorate is responsible through the Department of Employment to the Secretary of State for Employment.
c/f Employment service/Training and enterprise councils

Transactional Analysis (TA)

is a particular form of individual and group psychotherapy, which explores the ways in which people interact. TA utilises a model of studying social intercourse as a series of transactions. Its proponents

Transactional Analysis (TA)

regard each transaction as a ritual, within which each individual takes a 'position' as parent, adult or child. The analysis of the transactions explores the performance of roles, the way in which people 'play games', and the complexities of inter-relationships. Much of transactional analysis theory is based on the work of Berne, whose 1966 book *Games People Play* has been influential in social welfare circles.
c/f Psychotherapy

Transference

describes a therapeutic groupwork and counselling approach for re-living experiences, emotions, fantasies and memories from the past. It is primarily a psychoanalytical technique and is not recommended for use except by skilled therapists, since mis-use could be harmful for the individual or group concerned.
c/f Counselling/Groupwork/Therapy

Travellers

Travellers, including Romanies, New Age Travellers and others opting for a nomadic life style, have become the focus of specialist social welfare work. This includes working with travellers on official gypsy and traveller sites (governed by the 1968 Caravan Sites Act) and at 'park-ups' (illegal, or not recognised sites). Travellers' rights of access to an official site, education for their children and welfare benefits are subject to degrees of local discretion, which can result in discrimination and racial prejudice.
c/f Ethnic minorities

Treatment

With its roots in a pathological medical model of 'doctor', 'patient' and 'cure' 'treatment' has been viewed as a largely unfortunate and inappropriate term in social welfare circles. It is usually more acceptable to refer to treatment plans for offenders in certain categories, such as child abusers and sexual offenders, but social work assistance for others with problems, including victims, is more likely to be called *therapy*. In both cases, social work

Treatment (cont'd)

intervention would involve a planned programme. Treatment programmes, such as in Intensive Intermediate Treatment (IIT) have focussed on diverting individuals away from their offending behaviour.

c/f Intermediate treatment/Therapy

Trigger Pictures

are drawings, photographs or video images which can be used in training or counselling sessions to get feedback and discussion. Counsellors and trainers frequently need to explore the feelings and reactions of individuals in order to support and assist them. Trigger pictures are usually specially created to encourage responses. Special packs and videos, include some for use in training welfare staff to examine skills and work methods; and in social group work to respond to issues such as race, gender, authority, homelessness and poverty.

c/f Interactive

TWOC

is the acronym for the crime of *taking a motor vehicle without the owner's consent*. Social work staff along with police and others use the acronym as a word in its own right.

U

Unemployment

is the condition of being unable to find employment, when the person seeking the job is able and willing to work. Voluntary and statutory welfare agencies have organised a range of schemes to help the unemployed learn new skills and use their time in creative ways. Many social welfare staff are actively engaged in campaigning through political and community action, and have criticised the inability of successive governments to deal effectively with unemployment. There is also disagreement over the manner in which unemployment statistics are arrived at, critics arguing that the official figures disguise the size of the workforce who are out of work.
c/f Poverty trap

UNESCO

is the United Nations Educational, Scientific and Cultural Organisation, established in 1945 and based in Paris. With the moves towards a more European perspective in the UK, and various schemes to promote active citizenship, UNESCO may become a more important source of cross-cultural information on such issues as children's rights.
c/f Citizenship

UNICEF

has existed since 1946. It is the United Nations Children's Fund with a primary aim to provide social services, education and health services to children in developing countries.

Unitary Authority/Unitary District

The Local Government Act 1992, established a commission to review the local government structure in England, with a similar review having taken place in Wales. All the main political parties seem to be committed to a move towards unitary authorities responsible for most of the services presently provided through the county councils

Unitary Authority/Unitary District (cont'd)

and district councils. It seems likely that new unitary authorities will be established, but they will probably be based on new geographical boundaries, rather than either the district or county council divisions.

This *may* lead to an improved responsiveness to consumer needs, improved co-ordination of services and reduced bureaucracy. The new authorities might integrate health, social services, housing and welfare benefits functions, but, whatever happens, the purchaser-provider divide, with services 'buying' and 'selling' services to each other, will become more apparent.
c/f Purchaser-provider divide

Unitary Model

This model and theory of social work is based on the notion that social work should be provided in a unified framework. This implies that social work has a unitary purpose, and a set of methods that can be defined as one system. The approach was developed by Goldstein in America, and has attracted both converts and opponents in the United Kingdom. Many have argued that each set of conditions and problems faced in social welfare interventions is unique, and therefore a unitary approach is not flexible enough to be realistic.

However, the move towards more co-ordination of multi-agency services for users, and a more holistic approach to individual, community and societal problems may have developed, to some extent, from discussion about the unitary model of social work.
c/f Casework/Community work/Groupwork/Holistic/Multi-agency/ Social work/Systems intervention

User/User-led

The terms 'user' and 'user-led' have become synonymous with 'consumer' in most social welfare services. A user is seen as a person with choices, and is increasingly referred to as a participant in the provision of services.
c/f Client/Client-centred/Consumer

Validation

This term is used in different ways in varying social welfare contexts. Validation in training is the process of checking and verifying a piece of work, a skill or approach, or the standard of achievement attained.

Validation in counselling or group work is used by the worker to convey empathy and indicate that they are *really* listening and understand. For example, saying "I can understand how you feel", will be more likely to release emotion and tension than saying "don't worry, time will heal the problem".
c/f Counselling/Standards/Verifying

Validity

is a term used in social research to describe the method of testing the extent to which research is capable of measuring the quality or quantity it is supposed to be researching.
c/f Assessment/Evaluation/Research

Value Analysis

is the term used to describe an increasingly used method for calculating how good (or bad) the value of a service function is relative to the cost. The value of a social welfare service is found by adding up all the functions of an organisation, or by isolating specific functions and then dividing this by the relevant costs. So,

$$\text{VALUE} = \frac{\text{SERVICES}}{\text{COSTS}}$$

Britain as yet has no VA standard and relatively little application has been made of VA outside of quality assurance networks where it has begun to be used as a problem solving tool to obtain better value for money and quality.
c/f Quality Assurance/Value for money

Value for Money (VFM)

has become much vaunted as a term used to ensure
competitiveness and cost-effectiveness in the social welfare services.
The use of value analysis to obtain more quality effective and
value-for-money services has been applied to many of the ancillary
services subject to tenders, such as laundry and catering services. In
future, it is likely that more VFM incentives will be set for the social
care services in residential care and criminal justice, and these may
well be developed into the mental handicap and mental health fields.
c/f Quality assurance/Value analysis

Venereal Diseases

c/f AIDs/Sexually transmitted diseases

Verifying/Verifier

Verification is the activity of checking and approving that a job
has been satisfactorily accomplished. Verifying the performance of
staff, checking that outcomes are being achieved and constantly
monitoring procedures is a central task in social work to ensure
that standards are maintained. In the application of the National
Vocational Qualifications, the verifier is the person who monitors
the assessment process, ensuring that assessors are fairly and
consistently assessing candidates' 'critical enabling knowledge'.
*c/f Assessment/Critical enabling knowledge/National Vocational
Qualifications/Validation*

Very Sheltered Housing

is aimed at frail, elderly people, or people with mental health
problems, who do not need full nursing care, but do need a higher
level of support, care and supervision than ordinary supported
accommodation can offer.
c/f Sheltered housing

Victim Support

Various schemes now exist for helping victims or their dependants
who have sustained injury or loss through criminal activity.

Victim Support

Compensation may be awarded through the Criminal Compensation Board, which since the Criminal Justice Act 1988 can make a forfeiture order against convicted offenders. A National Association of Victim Support schemes exists, based in South London, which provides information, support and training on running victim support schemes. Many such schemes involve counselling self-help and mutual support groups.
c/f Compensation/Mediation/Reparation

Visual Impairment

c/f Blind and partially sighted people/Sensory impairments

Vocational Guidance

Offering careers and job advice is part of many social welfare employment remits. Preparing for work, filling in CVs, practising interview techniques and obtaining information on qualifications and training for different jobs are all assisted by staff involved in vocational guidance. This work can take place in formal settings such as social work offices, IT groups and schools, or more frequently in youth clubs, community centres, creches and mothers 'n toddlers groups.
c/f Employment service

Vocational Rehabilitation (VR)

All the different agencies involved in working with vulnerable people can become involved in managing and providing various forms of vocational rehabilitation. These include training and sheltered employment schemes, which can assist people who are mentally or physically disabled to become more self-sufficient and move into open employment where possible, do useful work and become less reliant on state funding and support. Vocational rehabilitation is an umbrella term to describe work-schemes, social education centres, adult training centres and occupational therapy and counselling and advice. With the implementation of the National Health Service and Community Care Act 1990, the support of people with disabilities in the community should be moved 'centre stage', with according

Vocational Rehabilitation (VR) (cont'd)

prioritisation of resources. Vocational rehabilitation does not belong
to any one service area, but lies on the borders of social work and
health and in specialist, mental health multi-agency teams.
c/f Employment rehabilitation service/Social education centres/
Vulnerable people

Voids

are a term used in both housing and social welfare to describe
'unfilled places'. In the housing context this is a vacant dwelling
for which no tenancy has been granted and/or no rent charged.
In educational units providing for special needs, the category of
'voids' are acceptable as a budget heading when dealing with local
authorities.

Voluntary Agency

is any agency or organisation which is not 'statutory', that is
performing a central or local government service as laid down
under legislation. Confusingly, many social welfare voluntary
agencies neither use volunteers nor rely on voluntary funds, but
either characteristic may be evident. In the partnership between
state, voluntary and private agencies, it is increasingly the voluntary
agencies which provide direct services for consumers, wholly or
partly funded from central or local government. The National Council
for Voluntary Organisations works to promote and protect the
voluntary organisations.

 Voluntary agencies are involved in almost every type of welfare
service and are particularly abundant in child care, work with older
people and the treatment of illness. Voluntary agencies frequently
act as pressure groups and complement statutory provision. Many
voluntary agencies have charitable status.
c/f Agency/Community Care/Multi-agency/Statutory services

Voluntary Associates

'Voluntary Associate' is the job designation for volunteers who assist
probation teams. They get involved in befriending and escorting work
with probation clients.
c/f Befriending/Probation and after care

Voluntary Transfer

describes the programme of 'Large Scale Voluntary Transfer' of
social housing (council houses) to housing associations, housing
action trusts and private landlords. The Conservative governments
of Thatcher and Major have encouraged local authorities to offer
their tenants the choice of transfer to other landlords or staying with
the local authority. The voting procedure in transfers has proved
controversial since transfer takes place if more than 50 per cent of
the tenants have voted and less than 50 per cent have voted to stay
with the local authority as landlord. The process itself was called
Tenant's Choice by the government.
c/f Housing associations/Social housing

Volunteers

Usually volunteers are people who give their time and labour to
help others without financial reward. However, in many instances
in social welfare work volunteers do receive at least expenses. The
range of volunteering is enormous, and the contribution to social care
likewise. Volunteers work in charity shops, youth and community
service, work with sick and disabled people, committees, courts and
in self-help groups, to name just some of the situations. In many
areas there is a local Volunteer Service Organiser and/or a Council
for Voluntary Service.
c/f Voluntary agency

Vulnerable People

Many different pieces of legislation relate to vulnerable groups
of people in society. These include, chronologically, the National
Assistance Act 1948, the Mental Health Act 1983, the Disabled
Persons Act 1986 and the National Health Service and Community
Care Act 1991.

The original 1948 National Assistance Act broadly defines
vulnerable people as people who have any kind of mental or physical
handicap. *Section 29* included, 'the blind and partially sighted,
the deaf and hard of hearing, the dumb, persons who suffer from
any mental disorder, and other persons who are substantially or
permanently handicapped by illness, injury or congenital deformity'.

Vulnerable People (cont'd)

Section 29 'vulnerable people' should automatically be able to get help from the local authority with general social work support and advice, access to facilities for rehabilitation and adjustment, and use of facilities for occupational, cultural and recreational activities. Sheltered employment and training facilities for handicapped, disabled, physically ill or mentally disordered people are provided *at the discretion* of local social services departments.

c/f Community care

Wardship

A ward of court is a young person who has been made a ward; placed under the protection and guardianship of a High Court judge. A judge assessing the child's best interests can make almost any order to meet the perceived needs of that child. Subsequently, any important decision affecting the child requires court consent.

   The 1989 Children Act under section 100 has restricted the use of wardship to cases not covered by statutory procedures (for example, Care and Supervision Order) available to local authorities. Previously, the High Court was seen as having inherent jurisdiction over all children as an ancient non-statutory (that is, inherent) right.
c/f Care Order/Child protection/Inherent jurisdiction/Supervision Order

Welfare Reports

Any court concerned with a child in a matter covered by the Children Act 1989 can order a welfare report. This may be compiled by a probation officer, a local authority or a third party, such as the NSPCC, working on their behalf. The report is expected to cover all the items in a checklist covered in sections 1 and 7 of the Children Act 1989. The court welfare officer may give the report verbally or in writing. If the court reaches a decision which disagrees with the welfare officer's recommendations, the reasons for the decision are usually given.
c/f Child protection/Court welfare officer/Pre-sentence reports/Social inquiry reports

Welfare Rights

The access to and availability of state benefits and services as a 'right' underlie the term. The right or entitlement to welfare benefits often exists, but welfare rights staff are often required to publicise the provision. Welfare rights have frequently become campaigning

Welfare Rights (cont'd)

territory for community activists and local authority or voluntary agency staff. The economic climate of the 1980s and 1990s has made 'welfare rights' a political football, with a new accent on the market-led economy on one side and a move towards empowerment of users through Community Care on the other.

As a form of work, welfare rights includes providing information on benefits and services, advocacy and counselling, and at times, campaigning. As such, it is often seen as part of a community development model of work. Specific welfare rights support is sometimes provided through law centres, welfare rights offices and the citizens advice bureau.

c/f Benefits/Community development/Community work/Welfare state

Welfare State

was originally used in the 1940s to describe the range of state initiated interventions designed to provide 'cradle-to-grave' resources to offset what Beveridge, in his famous 1944 report, described as the four common enemies: want, disease, ignorance and squalor. The social welfare services operate as the state welfare apparatus to provide financial supports through the benefits and social housing systems; education through schools, colleges and other training opportunities; health services through the NHS; and support, protection and assistance through social services, probation, prisons and police.

From the beginning of the 1980s, the move has been towards a pluralistic, rather than unified approach to welfare provision, with many local authority services being transferred to voluntary and private sector suppliers. Critics of these changes have called it the break-up of the Welfare State, whilst proponents have agreed that diversity of provision offers better quality care and consumer choice. The debate continues.

c/f Enabling body

Welfare System

is used in at least two contexts. One is to describe all the provisions and services provided by the State as public assistance to those

Welfare System

in need. The second, more specific use of the term, is in work with offenders, where the application of a welfare system, or approach, is in contrast to a justice approach. 'Welfare' means seeking full information about each individual offender, so as to provide an appropriate, individual response. Critics of the welfare approach say that it treats individuals in an inequitable way.

c/f Justice system/Tariff system

Withdrawal

Social welfare staff are often involved in a variety of community and institutional settings to assist drug users in coping with the effects of withdrawal from drugs. Withdrawal is the body's reaction to the absence of a drug which has been regularly taken, such as alcohol, a tranquilliser or a so-called heavier drug such as heroin. Withdrawal from different drugs takes a varying length of time, since there are both physical and psychological aspects of dependency. Some drug use creates permanent physical and psychological damage and past users have severe withdrawal problems. In other cases, withdrawal lasts only a couple of weeks and no symptoms persist. Drug rehabilitation programmes also are often referred to as drug withdrawal programmes.

c/f Dependency/Drug use/Tolerance

Withdrawal Symptoms

Drug or alcohol users can suffer emotional or physical signs of disorder when drug use is terminated after habitual use. Symptoms of withdrawal include sweats, shaking (DTs), mood changes and fear or panic.

c/f Dependency/Drug use

Women's Aid

Women's Aid is a self-help and campaigning organisation with separate organisations in England, Scotland, Wales and Northern Ireland. They work to provide temporary, safe accommodation (refuges) for women and their children suffering from physical, mental and sexual violence in the home. They also offer advice and support

Women's Aid (cont'd)

for battered women, and act as a pressure group to local and central government and the whole range of social welfare services, including social services and the police.
c/f Refuges

Workfare

is an economics-led proposal to solve the problem of long-term, structural unemployment. The idea was formulated in the United States, but has interested politicians and social planners in the UK. The proponents of workfare favour the gradual or total suspension of welfare benefits to able-bodied unemployed people. Instead, unemployed people would be expected to earn some or all of their benefits from participation in state and private or voluntary organisation employment schemes.

Workschemes

cover a range of projects and employment or skill training schemes aimed at people with disabilities or learning difficulties. Funding and management of such schemes have required a multi-agency approach, straddling health, employment and social services. Reality has often been different, with marginalisation of resources and lost prioritisation of resources. It is hoped that the implementation of the 1991 NHS and Community Care Act will improve the range and quality of services for vulnerable people in the community.
c/f Social education centres/Vocational rehabilitation/Vulnerable people

Workshops

are often used as a method of structuring smaller work groups at social welfare training events. The name implies activity and participation. Usually they are run by a facilitator and often they are arranged around tasks, themes or special interests. For instance, a workshop session may be set the task of solving a problem or producing a group decision or consensus, ending in a presentation. Workshops vary in length and size, but tend to last longer than seminars, usually lasting for at least an hour and a half.
c/f Buzz and cluster groups

World Health Organisation (WHO)

WHO was established in its current form by the United Nations with headquarters in Geneva, in 1948. Because many of the late twentieth century health problems are international, WHOs health education programmes, research and preventative programmes are of direct relevance to many social welfare staff. In particular, the impact of drugs and AIDs have raised the profile of health education as a universal, social and community problem, rather than being purely a medical concern.

c/f AIDs/Health education authority

Young Offenders' Institutions (YOIs)

are the places used for the detention of juvenile offenders who have
been found guilty of an offence in the juvenile court, renamed by the
Criminal Justice Act 1991 as the Youth Court. Very serious offences
may also be heard in a crown court or magistrate's court. The
regimes in YOIs vary but are meant to be "a busy and brisk regime.
The distinctive features of that regime will be a full and structured
daily routine; a grade system, greater emphasis on education and
physical education." (Home Office instruction 40/1988.) Sentences
last between two and twelve months and are available for offenders
aged from fifteen but under twenty-one-years-old.
c/f Youth court/Youth custody centres

Young People

c/f Adolescence

Youth Action

is an approach or style of work which empowers young people,
particularly those who are disadvantaged or seen to be 'in trouble' or
'at risk'. There is no one definition or way of making 'Youth Action'
a part of an agency's work with young people, but there seems to
be a consensus that a youth action approach includes: enabling
young people to be active participants; assisting young people to
understand and contribute to the working of organisations and the
communities in which they live; viewing young people in terms of
their strengths and potential.
c/f Detached youth work/Youth work

Youth Court

The 1991 Criminal Justice Act established youth courts to replace
juvenile courts. These deal with cases concerning under fourteen
year olds (children) and fourteen to seventeen year olds (juveniles).
Up to three magistrates sit at a youth court, and one must be a

Youth Court (cont'd)

woman. Sixteen and seventeen year olds are subject to sentencing as either juveniles or adults. For younger people aged ten to fifteen, the court now enforces parental responsibility, including their attendance at the court.
c/f Courts

Youth Custody Centres

Since the 1988 Criminal Justice Act, youth custody centres have been redesignated as young offenders institutions.
c/f Young offenders institution

Youth Service

The primary responsibility for the youth service rests with the Department For Education (DFE), but in reality, the service is a country-wide patchwork of statutory and voluntary provision. Resources for youth work are distributed patchily and direct statutory provision is often among the first service to suffer financial cuts. The National Youth Agency, established in 1991, out of the National Youth Bureau, has responsibility for the development of a core curricula for youth work, accreditation of staff training and general service developments.

Actual provision for young people includes facility-based and outreach work; activities and sports; special services for particular client groups – black youth offenders, girls, gay people, disabled young people, - and issue-focussed work, including employment, drugs, education, housing, personal relationships. Much of the UK youth service is provided through voluntary organisations such as Scouts, Guides and church organisations. Over 70,000 full time youth workers are employed and perhaps as many as one million part-time volunteers.
c/f Community education/Youth work

Youth Social Work

Social work interventions geared to meet the needs of young people are sometimes described as youth social work. This title was used by the specialist unit at what was the National Youth Bureau (now called

Youth Social Work

the National Youth Agency), to describe intermediate treatment and other community-based interventions designed to meet the needs of young people under supervision orders, or viewed as being at risk of offending. Groupwork, individual counselling, treatment, therapy and activity programmes can all be part of youth social work.

The term has also been used in Scotland to describe youth social work strategies in Lothian and Strathclyde regions, where integration of services between education, community education, social work departments and voluntary agencies has resulted in more co-ordination of multi-disciplinary and multi-agency services.

c/f Adolescence/Intermediate treatment

Youth Work

is the frequently used generic term for all work undertaken with young people outside of schools. Under education legislation from 1939 onwards, and especially post the 1944 Education Act, youth work was embodied in the 'service of youth' provided through a network of youth clubs and youth centres. The Youth Service was seen as a poor relation of mainstream education and it has consistently failed to consolidate its position as a central service. The main provision of youth work in the UK is made through voluntary effort in everything from the Scouts, Guides, Duke of Edinburgh's Award Scheme, through to church and ethnic-based provision. Social work provision for youth has been run alongside the Youth Service and relatively few truly integrated examples of multi-agency co-ordination of services exist.

c/f Adolescence/Intermediate treatment/Youth service/Youth social work